THE PLOT TO KILL HITLER

DIETRICH BONHOEFFER: PASTOR, SPY, UNLIKELY HERO

ALSO BY
PATRICIA McCORMICK

Never Fall Down
Purple Heart
Sold
My Brother's Keeper
Cut

THE PLOT TO KILL HITLER

DIETRICH BONHOEFFER: PASTOR, SPY, UNLIKELY HERO

PATRICIA McCORMICK

BALZER + BRAY

An Imprint of HarperCollins*Publishers*

Balzer + Bray is an imprint of HarperCollins Publishers.

Library of Congress Control Number: 2016936295
ISBN 978-0-06-241108-2
Typography by Jenna Stempel
16 17 18 19 20   CG/RRDH   10 9 8 7 6 5 4 3 2 1
❖
First Edition

To my nephews, Jack, Wisler, Champ, and Mychal

He who passively accepts evil is as much involved in it as he who helps to perpetuate it. He who accepts evil without protesting against it is really cooperating with it.
—Martin Luther King, Jr.

CONTENTS

CAST OF CHARACTERS

THE FAMILY

DR. KARL BONHOEFFER

Dietrich's father was one of the most prominent psychiatrists in Germany.

PAULA BONHOEFFER

Dietrich's mother was trained as a teacher and was one of the few women of her generation to earn a college degree. The Bonhoeffers lost two sons and two sons-in-law because of their involvement in the plot against Hitler.

KARL-FRIEDRICH BONHOEFFER

Seven years older than his brother Dietrich, he was a brilliant physicist and would go on to help Albert Einstein split the atom.

WALTER BONHOEFFER

Six years older than his brother Dietrich, he was an aspiring botanist. He died of injuries in World War I.

KLAUS BONHOEFFER

Five years older than his brother Dietrich, he was one of the original members of the conspiracy. As an attorney for a German airline, he used his ability to travel to build support for the coup. He was killed by a firing squad just days before the fall of Berlin.

URSULA BONHOEFFER

Four years older than her brother Dietrich, she married Rüdiger Schleicher, an attorney who was one of the original members of the conspiracy. He was killed by a firing squad just days before the fall of Berlin.

CHRISTEL BONHOEFFER

Three years older than her brother Dietrich, she married Hans von Dohnanyi, the architect of the conspiracy. Dohnanyi compiled proof of Nazi atrocities, a file he called the Chronicle of Shame. Christel was arrested along with her husband but released; she brought coded messages to him in prison so the conspiracy could continue. Dohnanyi was hanged at the Sachsenhausen concentration camp.

SABINE BONHOEFFER

Dietrich's twin, she married Gerhard Leibholz, a baptized Christian who came from a Jewish family. Dietrich Bonhoeffer and Hans von Dohnanyi helped them flee to Switzerland before they could be sent to a concentration camp.

SUZANNE BONHOEFFER

Three years younger than her brother Dietrich, she married the philosopher Walter Dress, a friend of her brother's.

MARIA VON WEDEMEYER

Dietrich's fiancée. After the war, she came to the United States and studied mathematics at Bryn Mawr College.

THE CONSPIRACY

ADMIRAL WILHELM CANARIS

Chief of the German intelligence agency, he originally went to Hitler to tell him about atrocities in Poland, only to find out Hitler had ordered the killings himself. Canaris then became a key member of the conspiracy and was executed at Flossenbürg alongside Bonhoeffer.

GENERAL HANS OSTER

Deputy head of German intelligence, he was Dohnanyi's superior and allowed him to hire Bonhoeffer and to collect information about war crimes. When those files were discovered, Oster was hanged at Flossenbürg alongside Bonhoeffer.

LIEUTENANT FABIAN VON SCHLABRENDORFF

A member of the conspiracy, he placed a bomb disguised as a bottle of cognac on Hitler's plane. He was arrested and tortured but never revealed the names of the other conspirators. He was moved from one concentration camp to another, including Flossenbürg, where he saw Bonhoeffer's body carried to an open fire. He avoided being executed at Flossenbürg because of a clerical error and lived until 1980.

MAJOR RUDOLPH-CHRISTOPH VON GERSDORFF

A member of the conspiracy, he activated a pair of bombs inside his coat while giving Hitler a tour of his headquarters; Hitler left unexpectedly and Gersdorff disabled the bombs. Because none of the conspirators ever revealed his name, even under torture, he was never caught by the Gestapo and lived until 1980.

CLAUS SCHENK GRAF VON STAUFFENBERG
A member of the conspiracy, he placed a bomb under the map table at Hitler's headquarters. The bomb successfully went off, killing four people; Hitler escaped relatively unharmed. Stauffenberg was killed by firing squad that night.

WERNER VON HAEFTEN
The young soldier who asked Bonhoeffer if he should shoot Hitler, he drove the getaway car for Stauffenberg and was killed by firing squad.

ARCHBISHOP GEORGE BELL
A member of the British parliament, he served as Bonhoeffer's secret contact in the British government. He was outspoken in his opposition to Hitler and delivered Bonhoeffer's eulogy on a radio broadcast three months after his death. Many years later, the Anglican Church acknowledged that Bell had abused children.

PROLOGUE

APRIL 5, 1943

The Gestapo would arrive any minute. Dietrich Bonhoeffer, waiting peacefully in his book-lined study, had been expecting this day for a long time. He arranged his files carefully on his desk and opened his diary to a page with fake entries to throw Hitler's men off his trail. Then he removed a panel from the ceiling and hid a letter alongside a sheaf of papers he'd stashed there earlier.

The purr of a diesel engine announced the arrival of a black Mercedes on the leafy Berlin street outside his house. Two of Hitler's secret police agents got out and climbed the stairs to the third-floor study. They told the blond, boyish-looking Bonhoeffer to come with them. He calmly said good-bye to his parents, put his Bible under his arm, and left.

Upstairs under the rafters was proof, in his own handwriting, that this quiet young minister was part of a conspiracy to kill Hitler.

Dietrich Bonhoeffer's desk and piano

ONE
A BIG, RAMBUNCTIOUS FAMILY

1906–14

Most of the homes in Breslau, Germany, had tidy front yards, neatly tended gardens, and thick Persian rugs in the parlor. But at the Bonhoeffer home, chickens strutted across the tennis court. Lizards, snakes, and rabbits were kept in a small zoo near the kitchen. And the family's pet nanny goat wandered freely in and out of the parlor.

The children—four boys and four girls—went to school at home, in a makeshift classroom with desks, chalkboards, and a trunk full of wigs, hats, and costumes. The family had a governess, a nursemaid, a cook, a housemaid, and a chauffeur, but their mother, Paula Bonhoeffer, was their teacher. She was strict when it came to table manners, but otherwise she loved to

Paula Bonhoeffer with her eight children. Dietrich is in the first row, second from left, and Klaus is in the second row, far right. Photographed in Breslau by Rotraut Forberg, 1911 or 1912.

say yes to her children's ideas. So when her oldest sons—Karl-Friedrich, fourteen; Walter, thirteen; and Klaus, twelve—asked to dig up the front yard to create an underground passageway, she agreed.

The boys tunneled all the way to the edge of the property, a stand of pine trees the children called "the wilderness." Meanwhile, the girls—Ursula, eleven; Christel, ten; Sabine, seven; and Suzanne, four—took over an upstairs room and turned it into a gigantic doll house. One time, they played all day—until the nursemaid rang the dinner bell.

They quickly washed and assembled around a massive dining room table. Everyone was present and accounted for—except seven-year-old Dietrich.

The nursemaid went out on the veranda and called his name over and over again. Eventually, his twin sister, Sabine, spotted him lying on his back, lost in a daydream in his secret garden hideout. He came in sheepish and sunburned, completely oblivious to the fact that he'd held up dinner. Again.

Dietrich was the dreamer in the family. His father, Karl, was one of the most prominent psychiatrists in Germany, and his mother came from an aristocratic family full of intellectuals. His older brothers were bigger, stronger, smarter, and, as Dietrich saw it, better at everything. Karl-Friedrich, the oldest, was a genius at physics. (He would later help Albert Einstein split the atom.) Walter could speak several languages, and he could identify every flower and tree he saw. Klaus, who their father said was perhaps the brightest of them all, was also the wit in the family. Dietrich's sisters were formidable, too. Ursula was a beauty, and, like her father, she studied psychiatry. Christel studied zoology. Sabine, Dietrich's twin, was athletic. And Suzanne, the baby, seemed to be good at everything.

Dietrich sometimes felt lost in this big, rambunctious, and talented family. He tried to do everything his big brothers did,

Home of the Bonhoeffer family at 43 Marienburger Allee
in Berlin, view from the garden

but because they were so much older, he was often dragged into playing dolls with his sisters. And so he would wander off to the garden to be alone. He would watch the clouds scud by overhead, feel the breeze rustle the pine needles in the forest nearby, and think. He would wonder: How did God create the world? Did God love everyone? Even bad people? Did God eat lunch?

But it was the sight of horses pulling a black-draped casket on its way to a nearby cemetery that set him off on a lifelong quest. From that day on, he became obsessed with a single question: What happens after we die?

Many nights, as he lay in bed across from Sabine, with only the glow of a small cup candle on the windowsill to light the darkened room, he would ask her if she could possibly imagine something as awe-inspiring as eternity.

"It sounds long and gruesome," she said.

If you believed in heaven, he argued, dying wouldn't be hard at all.

But for all his big talk, Dietrich was often afraid in everyday life. He was too nervous to walk home from school alone. He was terrified of learning to swim. And when a family friend dressed up as Father Christmas and surprised the Bonhoeffer children, Dietrich froze in terror, hiding behind Sabine's skirt.

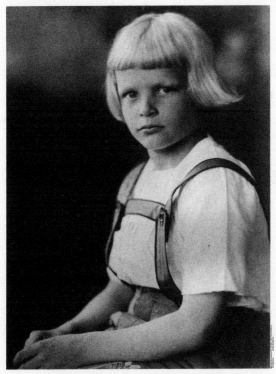

Dietrich Bonhoeffer, age nine, 1915

Sometimes he would summon up the courage to cut through "the wilderness" to visit his beloved grandmother, Julie Tafel, who kept an antique silver box filled with chocolate waiting for him when he visited. And sometimes while the others were outside chasing butterflies, he would plink away at the piano keys. Soon he was playing Mozart sonatas. By twelve, he was composing his own songs.

The whole family was musical; they gathered together many nights after dinner to sing hymns and folk songs. But Dietrich, it seemed, was a prodigy. Finally, it appeared he had found his talent. His parents arranged for him to take lessons from a demanding teacher and they began to think he would become a professional musician.

But his heart was never fully in his music. And so, for much of his childhood he remained the tag-along little brother. But someday, Dietrich—the little boy who was afraid of Father Christmas—would become best known for standing up to Hitler.

TWO

WAR BREAKS OUT

1914

Dietrich and Sabine were at a carnival on a hot August day in 1914 when their governess suddenly dragged them away from the horse-drawn merry-go-round. All around them the stalls and rides were being hastily shut down. World War I had broken out in Europe.

Like a lot of eight-year-old boys, Dietrich was fascinated with the war. When he was younger, he'd asked for pop guns and toy soldiers for Christmas. Now he pored over newspaper accounts of reports from the front. He tacked a map on a wall in the family's new home in Berlin and kept track of every move of the German army with colored pins.

War was exciting, even romantic, for a boy who followed

Germany's victories with pride. With his brothers away at school, now it was Dietrich's turn to drag his little sisters into games where they spied on enemy troops and stormed the ramparts—acting out the latest triumph of the German troops.

WORLD WAR I

World War I started with the assassination of the Archduke of Austria in Sarajevo. The Austro-Hungarians invaded Serbia, and Russia entered the fight on the side of the Serbians. Germany used the conflict to attack neutral Belgium and Luxembourg, then invaded France. The British came in on the side of the French, and a world war had begun. It would last for more than four years and result in almost nine million combatant deaths and more than seven million civilian deaths, mainly because of a protracted stalemate in France. It would mark the first time barbed wire and poison gas were used.

When there were food shortages, Dietrich became the family scout, scouring the streets to find out which shops still had plums and exploring the nearby fields for mushrooms. He spent his allowance on a hen so the family could have fresh eggs. And when the family went on holiday, the nanny goat was loaded in the train's luggage car, so the Bonhoeffers could have milk every day.

But his boyish romance with war ended abruptly when his

oldest brother, Karl-Friedrich, was called up for service. Now, suddenly, the war was all too real.

The Bonhoeffer family was well-to-do and influential; they could have easily used their connections to keep their son out of the fighting. But Karl-Friedrich saw it as his patriotic duty to serve. Indeed, he enlisted in the infantry, where the need—and the danger—was greatest. He left home as soon as he turned eighteen, taking his physics textbook with him.

When Walter left a few months later, he brought just one possession from home: his Bible. Dietrich stood by helplessly as his mother ran alongside the departing train and then stood weeping as it disappeared down the tracks.

Day by day, he followed his brothers' progress on his map, trying to reassure his mother with news of Germany's victories. One bright May morning, Dietrich, Sabine, and Suzanne were playing outside when a delivery boy arrived with a telegram.

Walter was dead. He had been hit by a bomb fragment and died of infection.

Dietrich could scarcely understand. How could God have let this happen? He and Sabine watched as their big, sturdy father bent over, his head in his hands; the children stood nearby, too frightened to comfort him. Finally, Dr. Bonhoeffer rose, and, clutching the railing with shaking hands, he went upstairs to tell his wife. Paula Bonhoeffer was so devastated, she lay in a darkened room upstairs for nearly six weeks.

After Walter's death, letters he'd written from his sickbed arrived, asking his parents to come visit him. The last one, written just hours before his death, said he was not thinking about the pain, but instead "longing" for his family "minute by minute throughout the long days and nights."[1]

The lively Bonhoeffer home became hushed and gloomy. Karl Bonhoeffer shut himself away in his study; Paula Bonhoeffer hid upstairs reading Walter's last letter again and again. Dietrich tried to cheer up his parents with his piano playing, but it was no use. He and his sisters tiptoed around the darkened house.

The eerie stillness of their home was broken when another telegram delivery boy rang the bell. Karl-Friedrich had been injured. A few days later, there was more bad news: Now Klaus was to report for duty.

His father was distraught, his mother inconsolable. They had lost one son, another was still on the front line, and a third was about to be drafted. When Klaus left to join the army, Dietrich would be the only son left at home. How could he show his parents that he was grown-up enough to help shoulder their grief, that he could take care of them?

On the day of Walter's funeral, Dietrich stepped up to the altar. He looked out at his heartbroken parents. Then he took a breath and sang, in a clear, unwavering voice, one of Walter's favorite hymns. His parents were touched by their youngest son's valiant effort to comfort them. But the Bonhoeffer family, which had seemed to lead such a charmed life, was shattered. Their father couldn't bear to be in the room if Walter's name was mentioned. Their mother fell into a severe depression. Dietrich was stunned. Now that death had come to his family, all his idealistic notions about eternity were thrown into doubt.

THREE
BONHOEFFER SEALS HIS DESTINY

1918–27

When the war ended in 1918, Germany had been crushed. The shelves in Berlin shops were bare, and the proud German people were humiliated by the terms of surrender. Karl-Friedrich and Klaus finally returned home—exhausted and disillusioned.

Dietrich was still feeling lost in a family where his older brothers were the ones who were expected to do big things. He wasn't the war hero Walter had been. He wasn't a genius at physics like Karl-Friedrich, who was now back at Berlin University, where he was a star student. And he didn't have the brilliant analytical mind that Klaus had begun to demonstrate at law school.

TREATY OF VERSAILLES

The terms of this treaty to end World War I had a devastating effect on the German economy and psyche. Germany was required to give up land they'd seized in Poland, France, Belgium, Denmark, Africa, and Asia. The treaty also required Germany to pay the victors for war damages they had suffered. The country's gold, ships, lumber, coal, and other natural resources were seized to pay these war reparations. As a result, the German economy ground to a halt and many people lost their jobs. Most humiliating, the Germans had to accept complete and sole responsibility for the war. These terms embarrassed and isolated the once-proud nation and helped created the bitterness that led to Hitler's rise to power.

Dietrich wanted to achieve something special all his own. Something that dealt with ideas more mysterious than isotopes and electrons. Issues more weighty than those in a legal brief. He knew what it was, but he was afraid his brothers would make fun of him.

Then a letter arrived inviting Dietrich to attend a prestigious music conservatory. For his parents it was welcome news: This could be Dietrich's first step on the path to a career as a concert pianist. They invited a well-known pianist to their home to hear him play. Dietrich desperately wanted to please his parents, but he knew he wasn't good enough—or determined enough—for a career in music. Their famous guest could tell, and so could his parents.

Finally, Dietrich confided in his mother. While he hated to disappoint her, he didn't want to be a musician. He was only thirteen, but he had found his calling: He wanted to become a minister.

It was an odd choice. Even though the Bonhoeffers were Lutherans—they said grace at dinner and family prayers at night—they weren't regular churchgoers. They were scientists and intellectuals. Men of reason, not religion. Dietrich's father, a prominent psychiatrist in Berlin, was perhaps the most skeptical of the mystery of faith. "I understand nothing of that," he once said. And he told Dietrich that he thought it was "a pity" that he would choose such a "quiet, uneventful . . . life."[1]

Just as Dietrich had feared, his brothers teased him. They told him he'd regret a career that meant a "retreat"[2] from the big issues of the day. A retreat? A life of faith was where he could really make a difference, he argued. The church was the one force that could prevent evil and truly help when people were in trouble. His brothers were unconvinced. The church, they told him, was a petty, feeble, bourgeois institution. Well then, Dietrich told them, he would change it!

Ever since Walter's death, Dietrich had been reading the Bible and other difficult philosophical books on his own. He had taken confirmation classes and started attending church regularly. He was so sure of his destiny that by age fifteen, he had started signing his name "Dietrich Bonhoeffer, theologian."[3]

Dietrich Bonhoeffer, age twenty-two, 1928

Only his mother seemed to appreciate his yearning for an explanation for the big questions in life. Although her husband and sons were intellectuals and scientists, there were a number of prominent theologians and philosophers on her side of the family. And so she went to church with Dietrich to try to understand why he felt so attracted to the ministry. As soon as she saw how devout he was, she knew that a life of faith was his destiny.

When he was confirmed she gave him a special gift: the Bible his brother Walter had been holding on his deathbed. Dietrich would carry it with him from that day forward, keeping it in his hands as he traveled the world for the next twenty years—ultimately bringing it with him to his cell in a Gestapo prison.

Dietrich Bonhoeffer would go on to become one of the most famous theologians in the world and he would write many books that would move people, even today, to fight for social justice. But he never explained why he became a minister. And he would always say that the roots of a person's innermost vocation should be private.

Perhaps his choice of a "quiet, uneventful" path was a way to set himself apart from the busy and talented older brothers who had always overshadowed him. Much later, Eberhard Bethge, his best friend, would think back to all the times that Dietrich had wandered off from his brothers and sisters to be alone with his thoughts. "It might be said that because he was lonely, he became a theologian," Bethge wrote, "and because he became a theologian, he was lonely."[4]

FOUR

LEAVING HOME FOR THE FIRST TIME

1923

When seventeen-year-old Dietrich Bonhoeffer stepped off the train at the pretty university town of Tubingen in the southern part of Germany, he was carrying his books, his pens and paper, his tobacco, and a hefty allowance. He was there to study, but he had brought along all the comforts of home to his apartment in this new city.

Finally, he would dive into the great philosophical mysteries with other students who shared his interests. Finally, he would meet learned men who would help him grapple with the big thoughts that had been spinning through his mind since he was a little boy. But he was also there to have some fun.

At Tubingen, he joined a fraternity known as the Hedgehogs.

At the Hedgehog lodge, he quickly became well known for his snappy wardrobe. Dietrich Bonhoeffer, son of an aristocratic, well-to-do family, loved clothes. Silk ties. Handsome tweed jackets. And handmade shoes. He may have wanted to be a theologian, but he would never dress like a monk.

He also reveled in the heady, scholarly atmosphere at Tubingen. He sat up late into the night debating the fine points of philosophy with his fellow classmates, and he impressed his professors with provocative questions. He challenged his professors relentlessly; some of his fellow students even saw him as arrogant. But no one doubted his intellect.

For his eighteenth birthday he asked for a trip to Rome. His older brother Klaus, who had just passed the bar exam, would be in Italy; perhaps Dietrich could tag along. His parents agreed, setting the stage for a trip that would change Bonhoeffer's thinking forever.

When Dietrich and Klaus boarded the train to Italy, they left behind an economy in tatters. Unemployment was rampant, and the German currency, the mark, was nearly worthless as the government struggled to pay back its war debt. A young rabble-rouser named Adolf Hitler took advantage of the turmoil and tried to overthrow the government. He was jailed the same year Bonhoeffer left for Rome. While Dietrich Bonhoeffer stood in a cathedral pondering the ways that faith can unite people, Adolf Hitler toiled in a jail cell, writing his manifesto of hate, *Mein Kampf.*

FIVE
THE TRIP THAT CHANGED EVERYTHING

1924

When Dietrich Bonhoeffer stepped inside St. Peter's Basilica in Rome on Easter Sunday, he was practically lost in a purple fog of frankincense. The altar was dripping with lace, the ceilings were encrusted with gold, and guards in garish orange-and-blue-striped costumes stood sentry in the corners. Bonhoeffer, accustomed to the simple wooden churches of Germany, was appalled.

At that time, it was very unusual for a Protestant to visit a Catholic church. Relations between the two faiths were distant, even suspicious. And Bonhoeffer was a member of the Lutheran Church—the first church to break away from Rome, in part because of the kind of opulence on display at St. Peter's.

He was about to leave when a young woman next to him offered to share her hymnal. He was so busy following the strange Latin text that he didn't take his eyes off the hymnal—until, as he put it, the "tender and melodious"[1] call and response of the congregation caused him to look around. He was stunned. He saw Italians, Russians, Greeks, French, and Britons all lifting their voices together. He saw a throng of seminarians, monks, and priests of every skin color imaginable. Suddenly, his own church, which was almost synonymous with being German, seemed small, provincial, and narrow-minded.

He scribbled something in his diary: "universality of the church."[2] These words would form the basis for a radical new idea of what a church could be. And it would be a belief that would propel him, years later, when Hitler was on the march, to turn to members of the clergy all across Europe and beg for help.

SIX

THE MEN WHO WOULD CHANGE BONHOEFFER'S FATE

1926

The Bonhoeffers' large, gracious Berlin home was adorned in garlands as men in evening attire and ladies in ball gowns floated across the parlor floor to the lilting strains of a Schubert waltz. A grand buffet had been laid, and outside a horse-drawn coach decked in white silk waited by the garden door.

It was Sabine's wedding day.

The groom, Gerhard Leibholz, had been a regular visitor at the Bonhoeffer home. A doctoral student in legal philosophy, "Gert" was beloved by the whole family, especially by Karl Bonhoeffer, who said Gert was his favorite of all the boys who called at their home.

As maids bustled around the parlor offering champagne,

Dietrich stepped outside for a moment. He looked in through the garden windows at his family. His oldest sister, Ursula, had already gotten married to Rüdiger Schleicher, a lawyer. And his sister Christel had married her former schoolmate, Hans von Dohnanyi, a government lawyer. Now Sabine had found someone.

As he looked on at the wedding celebration, Dietrich Bonhoeffer again found himself alone. Sabine had been his best friend. Now she had a new mate, while he was preparing for the solitary life of a scholar.

But it was through Sabine's marriage to Gert that Bonhoeffer would eventually face a crisis of conscience that would upend that quiet, uneventful life.

Gerhard Leibholz had been baptized as a Lutheran, but his father was a Jew. And even though his father didn't practice, his grandparents did. Still, Gert's religion was a nonissue in 1926— especially at the Bonhoeffer home. No one in the Bonhoeffer family had ever married a Jew, but many of their friends in the progressive university neighborhood where they lived were Jews. And many of Karl and Paula Bonhoeffer's friends were Jews who held top positions in academia, commerce, and the arts.

As Dietrich Bonhoeffer watched his family celebrate this happy day, he had no way of knowing the dramatic roles that Gert and his other brothers-in-law would play in his future. It was through Gert that Dietrich would first feel the sting of the Nazis' hatred of the Jews. And it would be through his other brothers-in-law, Hans and Rüdiger, that he would be drawn into the conspiracy to assassinate Hitler.

Dietrich Bonhoeffer with his twin sister, Sabine, 1939

SEVEN

A NEW IDEA OF WHAT A CHURCH COULD BE

1926–28

The doorbell rang, and the parlor maid at the Bonhoeffer home hurried to answer it before it rang a second time. "No visitors today," she whispered, closing the door as quietly as she could. The sound probably didn't travel all the way to the third-floor study, but she didn't want to do anything to disturb Dietrich, who sat there writing.

He was living at home again, studying at Berlin University. He was just twenty, but he was writing his dissertation at the same time as he took his regular course load—a demanding course of study for anyone, let alone someone so young. He wrote every day after going for a swim, working on a thesis that was both unconventional and, in the view of some of his teachers, naïve.

As he worked on his dissertation, he turned back again and again to his experience at St. Peter's Basilica on Easter Sunday. He drew heavily on the images from that morning to form his idea of a universal church—a church that could bridge all the differences among human beings. His Lutheran professors worried that he was too enamored of the Catholic Church and demanded that he defend this strange idea.

His dissertation, "*Sanctorum Communio* (Communion of Saints)," was a 380-page paper in which Bonhoeffer insisted that the church wasn't a historical institution; it was a living community that could transcend national, ethnic, class, and even religious boundaries. The "church" was not a building or an organization; it was a force for good, alive all around the world. The church should not be a remote, authoritative institution, he argued. It should be deeply and directly involved in the problems facing ordinary people.

In the end, his teachers were won over in spite of their doubts. He had written a trailblazing piece of theology, something radical and wholly original. He graduated summa cum laude.

But the idea of a church as a force for good wasn't just an academic idea for Bonhoeffer. He believed in this idea, heart and soul. And it was this belief in the church as a moral authority greater than any government that would put him on a collision course with Adolf Hitler.

EIGHT
FROM FAITH TO ACTION

1928

Dietrich Bonhoeffer, in a straw hat and linen suit, sat at a table in a sun-splashed Barcelona plaza drinking espresso. He marveled at the air, with its faint perfume of almonds, and at the amazing mix of people passing by. Rich, working-class, poor— they all mingled together, strolling leisurely under the avenue's palm trees.

It was a far cry from Berlin, with its chilly climate and strictly defined social order. And Dietrich Bonhoeffer himself was a long way from his old life in the stuffy halls of academia. After graduation, his father and his older brothers had encouraged him to go further in his studies. It would be a waste of his intellect to become a lowly pastor, they said.

But Bonhoeffer wanted to take action on his belief that the church should be directly involved in the lives of ordinary people. And since he was still too young to have his own parish, he'd taken a job as an assistant minister at a church for Germans living in Barcelona. He would bring his new ideas to his first parish assignment.

The congregation in Barcelona, however, was small and old-fashioned. Far from their homes in Germany, the parishioners clung to the old customs they'd left behind. They weren't all that interested in the energetic young assistant pastor with big plans for a new kind of church.

Bonhoeffer couldn't convince the pastor at the parish to try any of his ideas. He had a hard time finding people who were interested in the intellectually challenging conversations he loved. And the few times he was allowed to preach, his lofty sermons flew over the heads of the congregants. He lived in a ramshackle boardinghouse, alone in this foreign, friendless city.

Finally, he convinced the pastor to let him at least teach Sunday school.

The first week only one girl showed up. After that, Bonhoeffer went door to door visiting the homes of families in the parish, encouraging them to send their children to Sunday school. He was stunned by the poverty and hardship he saw—and moved by how much the parents sacrificed for their children.

Attendance grew at Sunday school, in part because the children were fascinated with the young, blond assistant pastor—and his funny Panama hat. And his linen suits. And the spiffy tennis whites he wore to play at the German tennis club. But he loved working with young people, especially the "lazybones, good-for-nothings, and early bloomers."[1] He had found his calling—and would find he always preferred the rough and tumble of working with underprivileged children to the pristine halls of academia.

Eventually, Bonhoeffer adopted the local customs, writing in cafés and having dinner at ten p.m. He continued his philosophical musings and wrote further about his idea of the "living church." But he was most excited about a plan that would take him even farther from his proper German roots. He put some money aside for a trip to India, where he hoped to study with Gandhi—and talk with the great man himself about how to put faith into action.

Back home, meanwhile, Germany had descended into further turmoil.

There were endless squabbles in Parliament, and many Germans wanted to return to a monarchy. Bitter and humiliated by the financial and emotional punishment meted out by the Treaty of Versailles, they longed for the glory of days gone by.

And they yearned for a strong, decisive leader who could lift them out of this national malaise.

Eventually that man would emerge: His name was Adolf Hitler.

NINE

GRAPPLING WITH THE EXISTENCE OF GOD

1929

A wet, slushy snow was falling as Dietrich Bonhoeffer arrived in Berlin. After months of sunny weather and outdoor dining in Barcelona, Germany seemed cold and dreary. And classes at Berlin University, where Bonhoeffer had enrolled in post-graduate studies, were dull. Worse than that, they started early in the morning. It was a tough transition from the languid life he'd enjoyed in Barcelona.

The one bright spot was a witty theology student named Franz Hildebrandt. The two young men had met at Tubingen and argued ceaselessly over the fine points of philosophy. Now that they were reunited, they griped about lectures that made them yawn and the doldrums of Berlin in winter.

They started off as classroom rivals, often taking opposite sides of an argument. Bonhoeffer could be quite stubborn. But Hildebrandt had a way of poking fun at him and at himself. After one debate where Bonhoeffer triumphed, Hildebrandt gave him a book he inscribed "to (my) ancient foe."

Over time, Hildebrandt would become Dietrich Bonhoeffer's closest colleague. He was Bonhoeffer's first real friend outside the family. And he was Jewish.

His mother was Jewish, so even though he had converted to Christianity—and had even become a Lutheran seminarian— he would still be considered Jewish when Hitler came to power. This would carry serious consequences for both men in the not-so-distant future.

But in the meantime, Bonhoeffer was working on another dissertation, one that sought to answer the question he'd been grappling with since he was a boy: How do we know that God exists? If we can't see him, what proof do we have?

It was an idea that great minds had struggled with for centuries. Is God a concept that human beings created? Is he the bearded figure on a throne of clouds? Or is God a spirit, present in each of us?

Bonhoeffer wrote about the proof of God's existence in the birth of a baby as a "whisper 'between eternity and eternity,'" and as evidence of a divine hand in "the power of what 'future things' will bring."[1] While other scholars debated lofty theories,

Bonhoeffer always insisted that God was real and present, not some kind of otherworldly phenomenon.

In his dissertation entitled "Act and Being," Bonhoeffer was critical of religious thinkers who believed that constant thought and reflection was a way to be closer to God; that sort of cerebral approach was what killed faith, he said. To be faithful, he wrote, a person had to be concerned less about himself and more about caring for his neighbor.

Again, his professors disagreed with Bonhoeffer's unorthodox thinking, but they had to agree: his writing was brilliant.

Even with two dissertations to his credit, at twenty-three, Bonhoeffer still was not old enough to have a congregation of his own. And so when he received an invitation to study at Union Theological Seminary in New York City, he took it. Not because he thought the best theological minds in America had anything to teach him. If anything, he thought they were a cut below the theologians of Germany. But ever since his experience in Rome, he was interested in connecting with members of other religions in other countries to test his idea of the universal church.

His older brothers had already been abroad, and they were lukewarm about Dietrich's plan to visit the United States. The first-class minds in science and philosophy were in Europe, they said, not in that upstart country across the Atlantic. Klaus was especially unenthusiastic about the idea of his little brother going to the United States, writing that he didn't think it would be a "decisive"[2] experience.

By now, the rest of Dietrich's siblings had settled down. Klaus had married a childhood friend, Emmi Delbrück. Earlier that year, his baby sister, Suzanne, had married a friend of Dietrich's, a fellow philosopher, Walter Dress. And Karl-Friedrich had married one of the Dohnanyi girls, Grete. Now, all of Dietrich's siblings were married. He was alone again as he set sail for the United States.

TEN

A DECISIVE EXPERIENCE: VISITING THE UNITED STATES

1930

When he crossed the gangplank to board the *Columbus*, Bonhoeffer was met by a crisply outfitted crew who showed him the lavish appointments of the ship. Crystal chandeliers, a library with cedar bookcases and leather chairs, a ballroom, and an outdoor pool. *Columbus* was the height of luxury.

On the first night of his trans-Atlantic voyage, Bonhoeffer settled into the elegant writing salon and opened his notebook. He reviewed all the American slang he'd collected before leaving—and he went over all the arguments he'd written down about why Germany wasn't solely to blame for the Great War. He might not have thought much of American intellectuals, but he did want to be prepared to debate with them.

One afternoon during the Atlantic crossing, while Bonhoeffer was playing chess by himself, a little boy about ten years old came up to watch. After a few minutes the boy asked if he could play, too. Bonhoeffer struck up a conversation with the boy, Richard Ernst, and the two became fast friends for the rest of the voyage. Once again, it seemed that Bonhoeffer was more at ease in the company of a young person than with the more elite travelers.

When the ship passed through New York Harbor, Bonhoeffer was impressed—overwhelmed, actually—by the soaring buildings. Richard Ernst, who lived with his mother in the New York suburbs, pointed out the landmarks and made Bonhoeffer promise to come visit once he was settled at Union Theological.

Members of the Union Theological Seminary, New York, 1930 (from left to right: Bonhoeffer, unknown, Marion Lehmann, Paul Lehmann, Erwin Sutz)

New York in 1930 was a dizzying, dazzling city—with many of its monumental buildings still under construction. The spire of the Empire State Building was reaching for the sky and crews worked day and night to finish the glistening new George Washington Bridge. Bonhoeffer had never seen a city so big and brawny.

He quickly dove into the hurly-burly of the city, visiting Times Square, Broadway, Carnegie Hall, and the Metropolitan Museum of Art. Occasionally, he took the train up to Scarsdale to see Richard Ernst and his mother, often bringing Richard a book or a toy.

Living in a dormitory was a completely new experience for Bonhoeffer—and he didn't like it much at first. The doors were always left open—intentionally, so the students would get to know one another—but Bonhoeffer was unaccustomed to and uncomfortable with this lack of privacy. He couldn't imagine how this noisy, chummy environment was conducive to serious scholarly thought and writing.

He studied with the best American theologians, including Reinhold Niebuhr—a firebrand who seemed to Bonhoeffer to lecture more about current events than about God. Coming from a strict German tradition of philosophy as a cerebral and spiritual discipline, Bonhoeffer was bewildered.

Americans, he wrote home, talked "a blue streak," often

"completely clueless" about the topic at hand. Everyone "just blabs away so frightfully."[1] Dietrich felt that his American counterparts were too interested in fairness to be really rigorous thinkers. He was, to say the least, unimpressed.

Then he met Frank Fisher, an African American student at Union Theological. It was the first time Bonhoeffer had ever had a conversation with a person of color.

Fisher would become a good friend, and he would open the door to the most formative experience Bonhoeffer would have in the United States. He took Dietrich a few blocks from campus to the heart of Harlem, the Abyssinian Baptist Church.

FRANK FISHER AND MARTIN LUTHER KING, JR.

Frank Fisher would go on to become a pastor in Atlanta, Georgia, and a civil rights activist. In 1957, he was arrested for sitting in the whites-only section of an Atlanta bus. Alongside him was a young Baptist preacher who had come from Montgomery, Alabama, to study how Fisher and his fellow ministers led their peaceful protests: Martin Luther King, Jr. The two men campaigned together in the civil rights movement and helped found the Southern Christian Leadership Conference, an important social justice organization. Both Bonhoeffer and King would seek out the chance to work with poor people. Both would lecture on the importance of faith in social activism. And both pastors would be killed when they were thirty-nine years old.

JIM CROW

In the United States, Jim Crow laws, state and federal statutes mandated racial segregation in public facilities such as schools, libraries, buses, restaurants, restrooms, and drinking fountains. "Separate but equal" facilities for African Americans were consistently inferior and underfunded compared to those available to white Americans.

The segregation Bonhoeffer witnessed in America caused him to write this letter home:

The separation of whites from blacks in the southern states really does make a rather shameful impression. In railways that separation extends to even the tiniest details. I found that the cars of the negroes generally look cleaner than the others. It also pleased me when the whites had to crowd into their railway cars while often only a single person was sitting in the entire railway car for negroes. The way the southerners talk about the negroes is simply repugnant, and in this regard the pastors are no better than the others. I still believe that the spiritual songs of the southern negroes represent some of the greatest artistic achievements in America. It is a bit unnerving that in a country with so inordinately many slogans about brotherhood, peace and so on, such things still continue completely uncorrected.[5]

Founded in 1808 by Ethiopian immigrants who severed their ties with the First Baptist Church in lower Manhattan when that congregation refused to seat blacks among the whites in their pews, the Abyssinian Baptist Church was now housed in a stately Gothic building in Harlem. As soon as the proper, bookish young German stepped inside, he was swept up into the singing and the dancing, the swaying and the foot stomping. The entire church, he would write home, exploded in "eruptive joy."[2]

The rafter-shaking music of the Abyssinian Baptist Church was a far cry from the subdued, ethereal chanting of the German Lutheran church. The pastor, Adam Clayton Powell, the son of former slaves, preached with the intensity that Bonhoeffer had been looking for at Union Theological Seminary. And the people in the pews cried out "Amen!" and "Hallelujah!" in reply. It was here that the mannerly, aristocratic Bonhoeffer found a spiritual home. Worshiping shoulder to shoulder with the congregation in Harlem, he would later say, was the only time "he had experienced true religion in the United States."[3]

He fell in love with Negro spirituals and began scouring the record stores of Harlem for folk songs, jazz, gospel, and blues. He spent hours at the New York Public Library to study up on the African American experience in America. He volunteered to teach Sunday school at the Abyssinian Baptist Church—and the congregation returned his affection. His students' families often invited the young German with his silk ties and tailored suits to their homes for dinner. And just like his experience with the poor families of Barcelona, he was distressed by the poverty in which they lived, but moved by the importance of their faith.

When Frank Fisher took Bonhoeffer south to visit his family at Thanksgiving, Bonhoeffer also got a firsthand look at the "separate but equal" conditions of enforced segregation. "The conditions are really rather unbelievable," he wrote home. "Not just separate railway cars, tramways, and buses . . . but also, for example, when I wanted to eat in a small restaurant with a Negro, I was refused service."[4]

Meanwhile, Bonhoeffer had another searing experience in the United States. One cold winter night, he and fellow seminarian Jean Lasserre went to see a film everyone was talking about. *All Quiet on the Western Front*, now considered an antiwar classic, tells the story of battle from the point of view of a young soldier. Horrified at having killed another human being, the young soldier holds the dying man in his arms and begs forgiveness. Bonhoeffer was moved to tears.

According to Lasserre, the boy who once loved play guns, toy soldiers, and war games became a pacifist that day.

Now Reinhold Niebuhr's lectures blending current events with spiritual themes made sense to Bonhoeffer. The more Niebuhr talked about a church that takes action—and doesn't just preach—on behalf of the underdogs, the more Bonhoeffer agreed. Bonhoeffer also had a chance to meet Rabbi Stephen Wise, an influential Jewish leader in New York. Although they couldn't have imagined it, Niebuhr and Wise would play key roles in Bonhoeffer's life as time went on. He would accept a lifeline from one—and commit his first act of treason with the other.

Newspaper reports of the Nazis' rise to power were already beginning to sow concern among Bonhoeffer's friends at the seminary. They urged him to stay on in the United States or travel abroad, but they begged him not to go back to Germany. One of them, Paul Lehmann, took Bonhoeffer to the docks to find a freighter captain who would take him to India, where he could study with Gandhi, but even with Bonhoeffer's savings, the trip was too expensive. Eventually, Bonhoeffer sailed back to Germany with an armful of jazz and gospel records. His friend Frank Fisher had one request. "Make our sufferings known in Germany," he said. "Tell them what is happening to us and show them what we are really like."[6]

Contrary to what his brother Klaus had predicted, Bonhoeffer's time in the United States was a turning point. He would say later that his experiences with the poor taught him to see life "from below from the perspective of the outcast, the suspects, the maltreated, the powerless, the oppressed, the reviled—in short, from the perspective of those who suffer."[7] "I turned from phraseology to reality,"[8] he said.

A RIGHTEOUS GENTILE

Bonhoeffer happened to meet Rabbi Stephen Wise because he hadn't known that tickets were required to attend Easter services at Abyssinian Baptist. But Wise had posted a sign outside his synagogue: "No dues for our pews." So Bonhoeffer went in and heard him preach.

Bonhoeffer has long been considered a candidate for the designation of Righteous Gentile, an honor given to those who risked their lives to save Jews from extermination. Stephen Wise, Jr., the rabbi's son, fought for Bonhoeffer to receive this award posthumously.

ELEVEN
HEIL, HITLER!

1931–33

His father's chauffeur-driven car was waiting when Dietrich arrived at the yellow-brick train station in Berlin in the fall of 1931. He was home from the United States and excited to be starting a new job as a lecturer and chaplain at the university, where he would introduce German students to the exhilarating music and worship style he'd come to love in New York.

But when he put up posters inviting students to a discussion about the role of the church in a country where the Nazis were coming to power, they were torn down. He printed new flyers and pasted them up. They, too, were ripped down. The night of the first meeting, no one showed up. While Bonhoeffer had been away in the United States, anti-Jewish fervor had crept

Dietrich Bonhoeffer with students from Berlin, 1932

through the campus. Students chanting "Death to the Jews" had assaulted Jewish students in one of the classroom buildings and had even thrown some of them out the window into the courtyard.

By then, Hitler's National Socialist Party, or the Nazi Party, had solidified its power. Preying on the bitterness that many Germans still felt as a result of the Treaty of Versailles and the punishing penalties the country had to pay, Hitler promised a return to Germany's former glory—and blamed the nation's problems on the Jews. The short man with the mustache and the bombastic speeches portrayed himself as the salvation that Germans had been waiting for.

Adolf Hitler at Braunschweig, Germany, 1931

In his theology lectures, Bonhoeffer gently reminded his students that the only real salvation would come from faith. And when he saw students greeting one another by shouting "Heil, Hitler," he spoke out against the idea of saying "*Heil!*" (Hail!) to anyone but God.

Still, he was happy to be back in the intellectual environment of university life. His students said he spoke so quickly and passionately that he could see them perspiring as they took notes. Soon, he became one of the most popular lecturers on campus; on any given evening more than two hundred students would be sitting at rapt attention, with others listening in the hallway. He posed deep questions to his students—and refused to let them off with "cheap and easy answers."[1]

Bonhoeffer pointed out that theology students would often ask if people still needed God. Bonhoeffer said this was the wrong way to look at faith. We shouldn't question God, one student recalled him saying. "We are the ones who are questioned . . . we are [being] asked whether we are willing to be of service, for God needs us."[2]

Even though he was a popular and charismatic teacher, Bonhoeffer felt a yearning to get away from lectures with privileged young people like himself. He thought back to his time in the homes of poor families in Harlem and knew what he needed was direct contact with those most in need. And so he decided to teach a confirmation class for teenage boys in a rough, seedy section of Berlin.

The first day of Sunday school class in the Berlin neighborhood of Wedding, Bonhoeffer climbed the open staircase to his classroom. He was dressed as usual, in a tailored suit and silk tie. A wad of paper hit him on the head. The remains of someone's lunch landed on his shoulder. Within minutes, garbage rained down on him. The boys hung over the balcony above, mocking him with a chant, as they repeated his name over and over again.

He walked into the classroom without saying a word. The boys followed him, still heckling the young minister.

Bonhoeffer went to the front of the room, leaned against the wall, his hands in his pockets. He didn't say a word. Minutes passed. The catcalls subsided. Finally, he started speaking—so quietly that only the boys in the front row could hear. The room fell silent, as the others leaned forward to hear him.

He told them they had put on quite a show. Then he told them a story about his time in Harlem, about boys like themselves, poor and overlooked by society. They were riveted. Bonhoeffer told them that if they listened he would tell them more next time. Then he told them they could go. He never had a problem with his students after that.

The boys of the Wedding neighborhood came to love and respect the young teacher with the patrician background—and Bonhoeffer, in turn, moved from his parents' wealthy home in Berlin to the boys' neighborhood so he could better understand their lives. He took a room above a bakery, and his hungry students often showed up just in time for supper. Finally, when the time came for their confirmation, Bonhoeffer realized that none of them owned a proper suit. And so he bought a huge bolt of wool and had suits made for each one.

He also wrote to Richard Ernst back in New York. He told Richard he wouldn't be sending him a Christmas sweater this year. Instead, he asked Richard to imagine the smile on the face of one of the poor boys of Wedding to whom he'd be giving it and to think of that smile as a far better present.

The Sunday of the boys' confirmation, Bonhoeffer took to the pulpit of the shabby little church. He praised the boys for their progress and told them that their faith now gave them courage that "no one can take from you."[3] It was, it turned out, the same day as a national election. As the boys and their parents sat in the pews, they had to strain to hear Bonhoeffer; outside, Nazi party officials drove up and down the street in trucks shouting campaign slogans through megaphones.

"GERMANY AWAKE," A POPULAR NAZI ANTHEM

Germany, awake from your nightmare!
Give foreign Jews no place in your Reich!
We will fight for your resurgence!
Aryan blood shall never perish!

All these hypocrites, we throw them out.
Judea, leave our German house!
If the native soil is clean and pure,
We united and happy will be!

We are the fighters of the NSDAP.
True Germans in heart, in battles firm and tough.
To the Swastika, devoted are we.
Hail our leader, hail Hitler to thee!

A few months later, on January 30, 1933, Hitler became the chancellor of Germany and christened himself the Führer, the supreme leader.

TWELVE

SPEAKING OUT AGAINST THE FÜHRER

1933

It was just after rush hour, when housewives were in their kitchens listening to the radio as they made dinner. Husbands were at cafés and coffeehouses enjoying a drink before going home. All across Germany, people were tuned in to hear a speech that was billed as a look at how the younger generation viewed leadership.

An unknown voice, soft, somewhat high-pitched, came on the radio. It was Dietrich Bonhoeffer, a twenty-six-year-old theology grad student. Just two days after Hitler was named Supreme Leader, Bonhoeffer denounced the idea of a leader who called himself a führer. Anyone who claims to be the supreme leader is ultimately what he called a "mis-leader," he said. And those who give total allegiance to a führer "will in the end be destroyed by him."[1]

Before he could finish, his speech was cut off.

The abrupt and eerie silence made listeners wonder: Had Hitler's men cut the power to the microphone? Or had Bonhoeffer run overtime on his speech? To this day, no one knows. But the question lingered: What would happen to a person who speaks out against the Führer?

The answer came a few days later. On February 27, 1933, Marinus van der Lubbe, a young communist, was accused of setting fire to the Reichstag, the government headquarters building. He said he'd acted alone, but Hitler claimed that the fire was part of an attempt to overthrow the government, a coup organized by a large group of his political enemies.

The day after the arson, Hitler convinced the president to suspend the constitution, giving himself sweeping emergency powers, claiming a threat to the country.

He suspended the parts of the constitution that guaranteed civil liberties. Hitler's men were now able to read the private letters of citizens, listen in on their phone calls, and search their houses at any time. Storm troopers roamed the streets, arresting and beating anyone who opposed Nazi party policies. Hitler also used the "emergency" to round up political opponents. His government then imposed the Malicious Practices Act, making it a crime to criticize his regime. And in a scenic little Bavarian town, the first concentration camp was established. The town was Dachau.

CONCENTRATION CAMPS

The first concentration camps were work camps, designed to hold political prisoners and so-called social deviants. Later, the Nazis created a system of camps specifically designated for the extermination of Jews and other minority groups.

Shortly after Hitler's appointment as chancellor in 1933, the Nazis set up camps to hold prisoners they considered enemies of the state: people who had simply spoken critically of the regime. They also imprisoned people they called "asocials": homosexuals, homeless people, and petty criminals. Prisoners were confined under harsh conditions and with no regard for legal norms such as arrests or trials. Soon they were put to work to manufacture ammunition and aircraft parts as Germany prepared for war. Often, they were arrested and disappeared with no word to their relatives. Many were literally worked to death.[2]

By 1942, the Nazis were rounding up all those with so-called non-Aryan blood—specifically, Jews and Roma people, who were then called Gypsies. These people also often died from overwork, starvation, disease—but many were systematically murdered in gas chambers. Nearly six million Jews and two hundred thousand Roma died in concentration camps.

THIRTEEN
THE ARYAN PARAGRAPH

1933

When Bonhoeffer arrived at his parents' home, his brother-in-law, Hans von Dohnanyi, was waiting for him in the foyer. Quickly, he pulled Dietrich into the study and closed the door. Dohnanyi, who was now a lawyer at the Supreme Court, had some disturbing—and secret—information. This would be the first of many occasions when Dohnanyi, because of his position in the government, would have access to inside information about the workings of the Nazi regime.

Any day, he whispered, Hitler's government would propose an amendment to the constitution called the Aryan Paragraph. All government employees would have to be of pure "Aryan" stock. Anyone of Jewish descent would be fired. Pastors with

Jewish blood, including Bonhoeffer's friend Franz Hildebrandt would be forced out of the ministry—into a separate church.

THE ARYAN PARAGRAPH

The Aryan Paragraph first appeared in the innocuous-sounding Law for the Restoration of Professional Civil Service. It stipulated that only those of Aryan descent, without Jewish parents or grandparents, could hold government jobs. Soon, it was extended in the Law against the Overcrowding of German Schools and Universities to deny education and teaching jobs to those of Jewish descent. Next it was broadened to ban even those married to "non-Aryans" from working for the government. Eventually, Jews were barred from jobs in the public health system, publishing, entertainment, and agriculture. Institutionalized anti-Semitism culminated in the Reich Citizen Laws, stripping those without so-called Aryan blood of their citizenship.

Dietrich had seen the effects of "separate but equal" in the United States, and even though he was just a junior lecturer at Berlin University, he knew he had to speak out. The rest of the country might have fallen under Hitler's spell, but Bonhoeffer thought that the clergy, men who had taken solemn vows to love and care for their fellow man, would take a stand against such blatant injustice. This, after all, was why he had become a minister, as he'd told his brothers back when he was thirteen—not to retreat from the issues of the day but to affect them.

As church leaders gathered to debate the Aryan Paragraph, Bonhoeffer asked for an opportunity to speak. He was only twenty-seven, but he was already known for his opposition to Hitler. As he spoke, the clerics fidgeted in their seats.

Bonhoeffer said that his fellow clergymen had a responsibility to question the government when it was in the wrong. This was a bold statement when Hitler's men were routinely arresting and torturing anyone who spoke against the Führer. Then Bonhoeffer went further.

The church, he said, has an obligation to "assist the victims" of government wrongdoing—"even if they do not belong to the Christian community."[1] He didn't say so, but everyone knew he was talking about the Jews. At that, some of the ministers in the meeting got up and walked out.

But Bonhoeffer had more to say. It was not enough to simply "bandage the victims under the wheel"[2] of the government, he said. The church had a duty to jam a stick in the wheel itself. He was calling on his fellow pastors to stop Hitler in his tracks.

Millions of lives might have been saved if Germany's Christian leaders had listened to the young preacher. But no one heeded his words. When the meeting ended, Bonhoeffer was snubbed by most of the others in attendance. A few days later, he was called in by his superior and told that any further criticism would be treated as treason.

While Bonhoeffer made a moral plea to the clergy, Hitler appealed to their desire for power. He told church leaders that he would restore the moral order that Germany was lacking. He also suggested that he would restore *them* to a place of political influence that they had lost since the days of the kaiser. He announced that his government would make Christianity "the basis of our collective morality."[3] All they had to do was swear allegiance to him and to the Aryan Paragraph.

Finally, church leaders gathered to vote on Hitler's demand. As storm troopers stood guard, a lone voice cried out in opposition. It was Bonhoeffer. But he was drowned out by jeering and catcalls. The church approved the Aryan Paragraph and installed Hitler's choice as their leader. Soon, they would hang swastikas behind their altars and pledge their loyalty to Hitler, crying *"Sieg Heil"* as they raised their arms in the famous Nazi salute. One minister declared, "Christ has come to us through Adolf Hitler."[4]

Swastikas now adorned every avenue of Berlin. Even Magdeburg Cathedral, an ancient cathedral in the heart of the country, flew the Nazi banner. The swastika, said one preacher there, was "the symbol of German hope. Whoever reviles this symbol is reviling our Germany. . . . The swastika flags round the altar radiate hope—hope that the day is at last about to dawn."[5]

SA and SS formations marching on May 1, 1936,
in the Lustgarten in front of the Berlin Cathedral

FOURTEEN

COMMITTING TREASON

1933

A line of storm troopers stood elbow to elbow blocking the entrance to the famous Kaufhaus des Westens, Berlin's largest department store. Nearby, pairs of soldiers patrolled the area with cans of paint, smearing the windows of Jewish-owned stores with a yellow Star of David. It was April 1, 1933, the day Hitler had declared a boycott of businesses owned by Jews. Anyone who defied him would be arrested.

Outside the department store, an elegant ninety-one-year-old grandmother in a white lace blouse approached the line of storm troopers. She would shop wherever she liked, she told the soldiers when they tried to stop her. And she strode past them.

That woman was Dietrich Bonhoeffer's grandmother, Julie.

That night, Bonhoeffer, along with his brother Klaus, arrived at their parents' home to meet with a pair of Dietrich's friends visiting from New York. Paul and Marion Lehmann noticed a change in their friend. He wasn't the carefree young man he'd been two years earlier; he was deeply distraught by the treatment of the Jews in Germany and felt he had to do something. The Lehmanns also noticed that every now and then, Klaus tiptoed to the door of the room where they were sitting to make sure none of the servants was listening in.

Before the Lehmanns left, Dietrich and Paul composed a letter to Rabbi Stephen Wise, the influential Jewish leader Bonhoeffer had met when he was at Union Theological Seminary in New York. They told Wise what was happening to Jews in Germany in the hopes that he would alert President Franklin Roosevelt. Under Hitler's new Malicious Practices Act, any contact with a foreign organization was illegal. Dietrich Bonhoeffer had just committed treason.

An incident in the coming weeks, though, would test his courage. It happened when his sister Sabine asked him to conduct her father-in-law's funeral. Sabine's husband, Gert, had converted to Christianity, but her father-in-law was Jewish. Dietrich was torn. He'd already been reprimanded by church elders after opposing the Aryan Paragraph; if he spoke at Gerhardt's father's funeral, would he get in more trouble?

Bonhoeffer went to his superior for advice. He reminded Bonhoeffer that Lutheran canon law prohibited ministers from officiating at funerals of the "unbaptized." If Bonhoeffer conducted the funeral, he said, it would create an uproar. He told him to decline his sister's request. It was a decision Dietrich Bonhoeffer would regret until the day he died.

His family didn't chide him, but his conscience did. "How could I have been so horribly timid?" he wrote to his sister a few days later. This is "something now that can never be made good," he said. "I must simply beg you to forgive my weakness."[2]

Before long, Sabine and Gert would face an even greater crisis. This time, Dietrich wouldn't let them down.

FIFTEEN
BONFIRE OF HATRED

1933

When Dietrich Bonhoeffer walked onto the university campus, he now had to pass under a giant swastika banner flying from the front entrance. Just about every one of his students wore the bronze Nazi badge on their lapels. And most of his colleagues had placed pictures of the Führer on their desks. Why hadn't he joined the Nazi party? they asked. He muttered an excuse. He knew now that he was working inside a nest of Nazi sympathizers; he couldn't trust any of his coworkers with his real feelings.

As he wrote to one friend, "If I no longer say anything about conditions here it is because, as you know, there is no privacy of post."[1]

His mother began to worry about him, saying he'd become

sullen and withdrawn. As his country—and now his church—embraced Hitler, Bonhoeffer daydreamed about the quiet, uneventful life he'd once hoped to have. And he thought again of going to India to bring Gandhi's ideas of peaceful resistance back home.

But by now Bonhoeffer had become a prominent figure in the church debate about the fate of the Jews. And he felt he had to stay in Germany to work within the church to convince the clergy that what Hitler was doing was wrong.

In April, the Aryan laws were expanded again; Jews were barred from working as lawyers and doctors at state-run institutions. In May, they were banned from working as university professors and notaries. In June, Jewish dentists would be fired from their jobs at state-run facilities. By fall, the ban would be extended to cover the spouses of "non-Aryans." And in September, Jews would be banned from film, theater, literature, and the arts.

One morning that fall, when Sabine's husband, Gert Lieb-holz, arrived on campus to give a lecture, he saw a line of students in Nazi brownshirts barring the entrance to the classroom, their jackboots straddling the threshold. "Leibholz must not lecture; he is a Jew," they said. "The lectures are not taking place."[2] Soon, word had spread all throughout the university town that Gert had "Jewish blood." Friends began to avoid the couple. Their daughters were shunned at school. Then Gert was fired.

THE ARYAN LAWS, 1933

- **April 1**—Boycott of Jewish stores begins.
- **April 7**—Jews are banned from practicing medicine or law in state agencies.
- **April 25**—Limits are put on the number of Jewish children who can attend school.
- **May 6**—Jews are banned from teaching at universities.
- **May 10**—Students burn thousands of "un-German" books.
- **June**—Jewish dentists are banned at state institutions.
- **September**—Spouses of "non-Aryans" are banned from state employment.
- **September**—Jews are barred from working in theater, film, and literature.

Adolf Hitler receiving the Nazi salute from a group of children, 1936

HITLER YOUTH

This paramilitary group was designed to indoctrinate children ages fourteen to eighteen into the Nazi philosophy and to recruit future members of the SS, the elite Nazi military guard. The members of the group held large rallies and performed in athletic contests. They were also used to break up church groups and spy on Bible study classes.

The young people enrolled in these groups, Hitler said, would be "a violently active, dominating, intrepid, brutal youth."[3] All young Germans were required to join; if they didn't, their parents could be arrested.

On May 10, 1933, thousands of students carrying torches poured into streets in towns all across Germany. They fanned out across the country, singing Nazi songs and chanting slogans against what they called "the un-German spirit."[4] Hitler's men arrived to whip them into a fury of hatred. At the stroke of midnight, they threw thousands of books into piles and lit an enormous bonfire. It was a grand "cleansing"[5] of "un-German" books—including works by Helen Keller and Albert Einstein. Also destroyed were the works of Heinrich Heine, a Jewish writer who had penned these fateful words nearly a hundred years earlier: "Where they burn books, they will ultimately also burn people."[6]

Book burning during the rally "Against the Un-German Spirit,"
organized by German students along with members of the SA and SS,
on the Opera Square opposite Berlin University, May 10, 1933

SIXTEEN
A NAZI CHURCH

1933

Adolf Hitler, a baptized Catholic, had once described Jesus as "our greatest Aryan hero."[1]

But now he decided that Christianity, which preached "meekness and flabbiness,"[2] was not in keeping with Nazi ideals of "ruthlessness and strength."[3] There was also too much emphasis on the crucifixion, which was "defeatist and depressing."[4] Germans needed a more "positive"[5] religion.

This new religion that Hitler had in mind would get rid of the Old Testament (which he considered too Jewish) and replace the Bible with his manifesto, *Mein Kampf.* The National Church would take down all crosses, crucifixes, and images of saints and replace them with the "only unconquerable symbol, the swastika."[6]

He urged the clergy to unite under one national church—the Reichskirche. A church where pastors and bishops would swear allegiance not to God, but to the Nazi party and to Hitler himself.

Under Hitler's plan, the Reichskirche, or new National Church, would immediately stop publishing and preaching the Bible and declare that the Führer's *Mein Kampf* was the greatest of all documents. They would also be required to remove all crucifixes, Bibles, and pictures of saints from the altar and put nothing on the altar but *Mein Kampf.* The swastika would replace the cross.

Church leaders were deeply divided. Some enthusiastically embraced Hitler's plan to strip all "Jewish" elements from their religion and to ban pastors with any "Jewish" blood, like

Bonhoeffer's friend Franz Hildebrandt. Others considered this heresy.

Hitler was confident he could turn the German church into a Nazi church. "They will submit," he said. Clergy "are insignificant little people, submissive as dogs, and they sweat with embarrassment when you talk to them."[7]

But a handful of these "insignificant little people," including Bonhoeffer, Franz Hildebrandt, and others, had begun to quietly fight back. They could scarcely believe that the church had not only failed to stand up to Hitler, but had now become an instrument of his oppression.

Bonhoeffer and the dissenters didn't want to create a schism; they wanted to form a wing of the church that would put allegiance to God ahead of allegiance to the Nazi party, one that would give aid to those hurt by the new anti-Jewish laws and one that rejected the Aryan Paragraph. More than six thousand ministers signed on to a protest letter written by Bonhoeffer and Hildebrandt, forming the Pastors' Emergency League.

Bonhoeffer sent out a letter warning this group of dissenting pastors to be on the lookout for undercover Nazi spies visiting their churches. He asked them to let him know immediately if Hitler's men tried to interfere with congregations. Somehow, his letter fell into the wrong hands.

On July 24, 1933, two Gestapo agents arrived at Bonhoeffer's door. Stop making trouble, he was told, or he would be sent to a concentration camp. Bonhoeffer was unbowed. He would soon take even bigger risks, but he would not put his fellow pastors in harm's way. He told his fellow dissenters to destroy all leaflets critical of the Reichskirche and try to keep ministering to their parishes under the new constraints.

That fall, some leaders of Hitler's new church staged a rally at a huge sports arena. Under a banner that read "One Reich. One People. One Church," more than twenty thousand people gathered to pledge allegiance to the new Nazi religion, the Reichskirche.

SEVENTEEN
A DIFFERENT KIND OF RESISTANCE

1933–34

Dietrich Bonhoeffer sat alone in a damp, dreary apartment in London, feeding coins into a small gas heater. Demoralized, increasingly isolated from his church, and frustrated with his inability to rally the clergy against Hitler, he had accepted a post at a German parish in London.

Before he left, his superiors told him to take back his criticism of the Reichskirche. Instead, Bonhoeffer requested a meeting with Bishop Ludwig Müller, the head of Hitler's new church. When Müller demanded that he remove his signature from the Pastors' Emergency League petition, Bonhoeffer refused. When he tried to explain why, Müller cut him off and sent him away.

Bonhoeffer had moved to London to make a statement: He

would not be part of a church that didn't stand up for the Jews. He also told friends that he would use the time to reflect on his future. And so, as he sat in his chilly apartment, he thought and thought, just as he had as a boy in his backyard.

He loved the church. He had committed his life to it. And he had tried to reform it, as he had promised his brothers long ago. Would he walk away from the church now that it was the Nazi church? Or did the church need him now more than ever? He was an avowed pacifist, a lowly junior pastor. But a dangerous new question had begun to take shape in his mind: Was there another way he could fight Hitler? Bonhoeffer wrote to his friend Hildebrandt, telling him he was beginning to think that something greater would be required of him: a different kind of resistance. "A 'resistance unto death.'"[1]

As he grappled with what shape this resistance would take, he turned for comfort to his favorite New Testament passage, the Sermon on the Mount. He wondered: What did it really mean to be a disciple of Christ? He stayed up late into the night writing. Listening to God was not enough, he wrote. To be a true disciple, a person has to act. Or, as Jesus said to his disciples, a man must "take up his cross and follow me." (Matthew 16:24)

He was keenly aware of the next Gospel verse. "For whoever wishes to save his life will lose it; but whoever loses his life for my sake will find it." (Matthew 16:25)

From all outward appearances, Bonhoeffer was ministering

to a lower-class parish of butchers' and bakers' families by day and writing a weighty theological treatise in his apartment by night. And by now Hildebrandt had resigned his post as a parish priest to protest the Nazi interference in the church and had fled to London, where he joined Bonhoeffer. The two of them went to museums and concerts and appeared to be having a great time. But Bonhoeffer had already begun to take up a new form of resistance.

Through a series of connections, he made secret contact with a powerful member of the House of Lords, Archbishop George Bell. Bell had kept his distance from the official representatives of the German church in England, but he liked the mannerly young Bonhoeffer. And he listened intently as Bonhoeffer told him about the Nazi campaign to take over the church. He told him about the impact of the Aryan laws. And he asked Bell to use his position as a member of Parliament to speak out.

Bell created a stir when he wrote a letter to the *Times* of London and an editorial for an influential religious journal laying out the ways the Nazis had corrupted the church. He also wrote to religious leaders in other countries, asking them to speak out against the Nazis. Back in Germany, Hitler's men were furious. Who had gone to this British official behind their backs? To conspire with a foreign government—especially one of the enemies that had defeated Germany in the Great War—wasn't just dangerous. According to the Malicious Practices Act, the measure that granted emergency powers to Hitler, it was treason.

CONTROLLING THE CHURCH

In an effort to cover up the division within the church, a law was passed declaring that discussions about the church could only take place inside churches. Members of the clergy were prevented from talking to the press; if they did, they would be kicked out of the church. All church youth groups would now be required to become chapters of Hitler Youth.

They quickly discovered the source of the information: It was that meddlesome young minister, Dietrich Bonhoeffer.

Soon, Bonhoeffer received an urgent demand from his superior. He was to return to Berlin immediately. When Bonhoeffer sat down at a long wooden table in the offices of the Reichskirche in Berlin, the bishop placed a document in front of him and told him to sign it. It was a pledge of compliance, an agreement to refrain from any contact with other churches or any speech critical of the regime.

Bonhoeffer studied the pledge in front of him. He had come home to meet with the bishop, as demanded; that act, he vowed to himself, would be "his last act of obedience"[2] to the church. He pushed the piece of paper back across the table and left the room.

EIGHTEEN
NIGHT OF THE LONG KNIVES

1934

A letter on rough, cream-colored stationery was waiting for Bonhoeffer when he came home on a crisp November day. "Dear friend," it said. "You can come whenever you like. The sooner the better . . . You will be staying with me if I am out of prison and . . . if you can live on the simple vegetarian food . . . you will have nothing to pay for your boarding and lodging."[1]

It was signed "MK Gandhi."

Finally, Bonhoeffer would get to sit at the feet of the great teacher of nonviolent resistance. He had been studying Gandhi's methods for a long time and now believed that Hitler might be stopped by using those same techniques in Germany. His friends and mentors disagreed, saying the passive resistance put forth by Gandhi was no match for the brutality of the Nazis. But Bonhoeffer said the exact opposite was true. The future of his church—and his nation—depended on answering that brutality with such gentle ways. "It sometimes seems to me that there's more Christianity in [India's] 'heathenism' than in the whole of our Reichskirche,"[2] he said.

The timing of the trip was ideal. He would leave the next fall and miss the cold Berlin winter. More important, he would be far from the sights of the Nazis. And that past summer, Hitler's men had shown just how far they would go to silence those who opposed them.

Back on June 29, 1934, while Berlin slept, storm troopers roamed the streets. Men and women were dragged out of bed. Some were shot in their own homes; others died by firing squads in back alleys. Most were political opponents who'd spoken out against the Führer; two were generals who had simply disagreed with him. By the time the sun rose, after what would be called the Night of the Long Knives, Hitler announced that the raids had been necessary to stop a threat to his own life. He said seventy-four people had been shot. But Dohnanyi, through his secret sources, found evidence that more than two hundred people had been murdered. He couldn't prove it, but it was possible that as many as a thousand people had been killed or hauled off to concentration camps.

THE NUREMBERG LAWS

In 1935 the Nuremberg Laws were passed. Called the Laws for the Protection of German Blood and German Honor, they stated that "the purity of German blood is essential to the further existence of the German people," and set out these new laws:

- Marriages between Jews and citizens of German blood are forbidden.
- Extramarital intercourse between Jews and subjects of the German state are forbidden.
- Jews will not be permitted to employ female citizens of German or kindred blood as domestic workers under the age of forty-five.[3]

Later that summer, the German president, Paul von Hindenburg, a revered war hero, passed away. It was an emotional and patriotic moment when Hitler summoned his troops to a garrison in Berlin in the middle of the night. By flickering torchlight, he asked the grieving soldiers to renew their oath of allegiance. But when they raised their hands, they found themselves swearing an oath of unconditional obedience not to their country but to Adolf Hitler himself.

NINETEEN

A BREAKAWAY CHURCH

1934–37

A ramshackle house surrounded by small buildings with thatched roofs stood nearly hidden in the dunes of the German seacoast. A mile from town, it couldn't be seen from any of the neighboring farms. It was the perfect place for Bonhoeffer to work, far from the prying eyes of the Nazis, on the founding declaration for a new church. One that would "speak out for those who cannot speak."[1]

He had come to the seaside town of Zingst with meager funds from the Pastors' Emergency League and a handful of idealistic young theology students to create a seminary for the new Confessing Church. Together they painted the walls, scrubbed the floors, and repaired the roof. Bonhoeffer threw himself into the work, even though he had agonized about his new mission. He had given up the chance to study with Gandhi. He had given up the safety of London. But he would not give up on the church—or at least on creating a new wing that would speak so loudly against Hitler that the rest of the world would have to listen.

THE 1936 OLYMPIC GAMES

When Germany was selected to host the Olympics in 1936, Hitler initially tried to prohibit Jews and blacks from participating. He saw the games as a chance to showcase a "new Germany" and the Aryan master race. But US track-and-field star Jesse Owens, an African American athlete, was the star of the games, winning four gold medals; the German track team won only one. Bonhoeffer attended the games but was not in the stands on the day of Owens's victory.

"Perhaps I seem to you rather fanatical," he wrote to his brother Karl-Friedrich. "I myself am sometimes afraid of that. . . . Things do exist that are worth standing up for without compromise. To me it seems that peace and social justice are such things."[2]

Later the seminary would move to an abandoned estate in

the hills of Pomerania. In this idyllic setting, the men read, meditated, did manual labor, and listened to Bonhoeffer's Negro spirituals. He was the leader of the community—and still a sporty dresser, in his linen suits and silk ties, but he insisted on being called "brother," just like the others. By day, he put them through rigorous studies, led the choir, and played soccer with them; by night, he worked on his call to action for the formation of a new church—one that would directly challenge Adolf Hitler.

That piece of writing would become a book called *The Cost of Discipleship*. It is a book that has gone down in history as one of the most important religious texts ever written. It is not enough to simply believe in God, Bonhoeffer says. That is "cheap grace."[3] One must take actions based on that belief.

Bonhoeffer urged the members of the new Confessing Church to adopt a mission statement that would declare their opposition to the Nazis. The Pastors' Emergency League debated and debated. But they could not take such a bold step.

Bonhoeffer was bitterly disappointed. Meanwhile, he received a letter from Berlin University. He had been fired. Furthermore, he was prohibited from all teaching or public speaking in Berlin. Then he got word that Franz Hildebrandt had been arrested. Bonhoeffer and some friends got

Hildebrandt released and quickly spirited out of the county.

But Bonhoeffer would not give up. Quickly, he set out on a trip through Europe, asking church leaders in Italy, France, and Switzerland to intervene in Germany. He begged. He pleaded. Please, he asked his fellow ministers, do something. But none of them would take a stand against Hitler. He wrote to his friend Eberhard Bethge around this time, saying he was suffering a deep "sadness of the heart."[4]

EVENTS OF 1935–37

- September 1935—The Nuremberg Laws are passed, safeguarding the purity of "German blood and German honor."
- August 1936—Olympic Games are held in Berlin.
- December 1936—All German children are required to join the Hitler Youth.
- July 1937—Martin Niemöller, a leading cleric critical of Hitler, is arrested.

TWENTY
A CONSPIRACY BEGINS

1937–38

Hans von Dohnanyi, Dietrich's brother-in-law, had become edgy and secretive. The whole family, gathered for dinner at their parents' home, had noticed. Usually, after the meal, he and Klaus went into the study to talk. Tonight, he took Dietrich aside. He needed advice. It was an ethical question, he said.

At dinner that evening, the conversation had been grim. Unless the Nazi regime was stopped, Germany would plunge into war, they all agreed. Some people they knew—wealthy, well-connected Germans—were leaving the country. Political prisoners were being rounded up in the middle of the night and disappearing. The old, the sick, and the disabled were being described as "useless eaters" or "life unworthy of life."[1] What had become of their country? What should they do?

As the conversation swirled around him, Hans was silent. Later he confided in Dietrich.

He had bad news, news that would affect Sabine and Gert. Because of his job in the Justice Ministry, Dohnanyi had advance information about a new restriction that would be imposed on Jews. The passports of all those of Jewish descent would soon be stamped with the letter *J*, meaning they could not leave the country.

He also explained why he'd become so secretive. In a locker hidden in a town about twenty miles outside Berlin, he'd amassed a collection of documents, photographs, and witness statements about the Nazis' abuse of power. He had proof of the disappearance of political enemies, Jews, and others. Detailed records of the arrests and torture. Proof of the ways that Hitler's underlings had swindled Jewish citizens out of possessions and money. The files were a record he called the Chronicle of Shame.

Then he told Bonhoeffer a secret that would change his life: Dohnanyi and a small band of conspirators, including Klaus Bonhoeffer, Rüdiger Schleicher (Bonhoeffer's brother-in-law), and others were plotting to overthrow Hitler. The conspirators were patriotic men who took their oath of allegiance to Germany very seriously. They knew they would be killed if they committed treason, but they were willing to take the risk.

But Dohnanyi had a question for his brother-in-law, the theologian: Was it a sin to commit treason?

Bonhoeffer told him that he and the other conspirators would indeed be subject to God's judgment for their actions. But, he said, God would forgive whatever sins they had to undertake to stop a madman. "Silence in the face of evil is itself evil," he would later write. "Not to speak is to speak. Not to act is to act."[2]

Bonhoeffer had given Dohnanyi and the other members of the conspiracy the spiritual fortitude and moral justification to act. But he was an avowed pacifist, dedicated to peaceful resistance; he still didn't know what *his* role should be.

MEMBERS OF THE CONSPIRACY

The innermost circle of the conspiracy was led by Hans von Dohnanyi, Bonhoeffer's brother-in-law, who was first a lawyer at the Supreme Court and later an official at the Abwehr, the German intelligence agency. In his position, he had early notice of the Aryan laws; later he collected a detailed file of Nazi atrocities. Klaus Bonhoeffer, an attorney at the German airline Lufthansa, used his position to travel to other countries to try to build support for the overthrow of Hitler. Rüdiger Schleicher, who was married to Ursula Bonhoeffer, was an aviation official; his role was to secure safe air travel for the new government after the coup. Dietrich Bonhoeffer was a courier and spy for the resistance and was the moral conscience of the group.

Bonhoeffer family home, site of conspiracy meetings

TWENTY-ONE
THE WAR HITS HOME

1938

By 1938 Hitler's war machine had roared to life. His army rolled into Austria and annexed its territory, effectively making Austria part of Germany. Next, he set his sights on Czechoslovakia. Soon all of Europe would be engulfed in the flames of war, and thousands of young German men would be called up to fight. Including the seminarians of the Confessing Church.

Out on a walk one day, the young men under Bonhoeffer's tutelage debated the issue. Then one of young men turned to Bonhoeffer for advice. What would *he* do if he were drafted? Bonhoeffer was silent for a long time, as he stooped and let a handful of sand sift through his fingers.

His brothers had fought for Germany, and Bonhoeffer considered himself a patriot. But he was also a pacifist.

Finally, he stood and said, "I pray that God will give me the strength not to take up arms."[1]

As he struggled with his own course of action, Bonhoeffer urged the members of the Confessing Church and the Pastors' Emergency League to give up the safety and comfort of parish life and fight for peace. "There is no way to peace along the way of safety," he said in a speech. "Peace must be dared, it is itself the great venture and can never be safe."[2]

Bonhoeffer had already taken a risk by funneling information to Archbishop George Bell in England and by meeting with leaders of other churches in Europe. Now he was calling on his fellow pastors to join him. "What are we waiting for?" he said. "The time is late."[3] But once again, his pleas fell on deaf ears. The members of the Confessing Church would go only so far: They would condemn Hitler's interference with religious matters, but they would not take action to help the Jews. Bonhoeffer was crushed.

Not long after that speech, on January 11, 1938, Bonhoeffer was arrested. The Gestapo interrogated him for seven hours before releasing him. He was put on a train and banned from Berlin. The little seminary in the hills was shut down.

Now Sabine turned to him for help. The law requiring Jews to hold special passports was about to go into effect. If she and her family were going to escape, they had to go soon. But where would they go?

Early one morning, Sabine told her two daughters that the family was going away for the weekend with their uncle Dietrich. They packed their car lightly, but the girls were told to wear two sets of underwear since they wouldn't be back till Monday. Bonhoeffer sang songs to keep the girls distracted as the trip wore on. Eventually, they stopped at a grassy spot by the side of the road for a picnic. Then Bonhoeffer put Sabine and her family back in the car and sent them on. He waved good-bye as the car headed to the Swiss border. Dietrich, through his contacts in the Swiss church, had gotten them to safety. From there, they would go to live in England, with help from Archbishop Bell. They would survive the war in safety.

When Bonhoeffer got back home, a letter was waiting for him. He was to register with the military immediately.

Bonhoeffer prayed for guidance. If he declared himself a conscientious objector, he would be arrested and executed. If he refused to fight, the young seminarians might think he expected them to follow his lead—and they, too, would be killed. How could he obey his own conscience but not risk the lives of others?

While he agonized, others were taking actions on his behalf. Unbeknownst to him, family members and church leaders were arranging for him to go back to the United States. Reinhold Niebuhr, his old professor at Union Theological Seminary, appealed to officials there, telling them that if they didn't make room for Bonhoeffer, he would end up in a concentration camp.

Hans von Dohnanyi also pulled some strings. He wanted to save his brother-in-law, but he also wanted to preserve Bonhoeffer's secret ties to Bell and the British government. And perhaps he could spread the word in the United States of Hitler's wrongdoings.

By the time he was due to report for service in Hitler's army, Dietrich Bonhoeffer was on an ocean liner on his way to America.

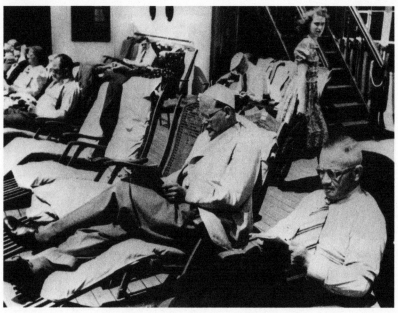

Dietrich Bonhoeffer on a ship traveling to America, summer 1939

TWENTY-TWO
A DARK NIGHT OF THE SOUL

1939

All the lights were out in the dorms at Union Theological Seminary. All but one—the desk lamp in the prophet's corner, an ornate wood-paneled room reserved for VIPs. There sat Dietrich Bonhoeffer, an overflowing ashtray on his desk, a small fan blowing a feeble breeze in his direction, as he crumpled up another paper and threw it in the waste can. New York was in the grip of a beastly heat wave and Bonhoeffer was miserable. He couldn't think. He couldn't write. He could barely concentrate enough to read his Bible.

He'd arrived to a warm welcome at his old school a few days earlier. He'd been invited for a weekend in the country at the home of Henry Sloane Coffin, the president of the seminary, who'd helped create a position there that would allow Bonhoeffer to safely sit out the war. But Dietrich was instantly sick with regret. He knew that many people had gone to extraordinary lengths on his behalf, but, as he wrote in his diary, he didn't know why he was in the United States when he could have been back in Germany being useful.

He wandered down to Times Square and stared at the newsreel for an hour, desperately looking for news about Germany. He took a day trip to the World's Fair, nearby in Queens, if only to get lost in the crowds. But he quickly retreated to his room to think. "One is less lonely when one is alone,"[1] he wrote in his diary. And one night, Bonhoeffer sat alone in the common room holding a cup of cold coffee between his hands. As lively conversation swirled around him, Bonhoeffer muttered, "I shouldn't be here."[2]

Now he was alone in a stifling dorm room, "in utter despair."[3] He opened his Bible. "The one who believes does not flee," it said. (Isaiah 28:16)

It was the sign he had been waiting for. He would go home immediately. "It is cowardice and weakness to run away here now,"[4] he wrote in his diary. He hated to disappoint those who had worked so hard on his behalf, but he knew his place was in Germany, not in the safety of the United States. "It probably means more for me than I can see at the moment. God alone knows what."[5]

BONHOEFFER'S DIARY

June 15, 1939.

Since yesterday evening I haven't been able to stop thinking of Germany. I would not have thought it possible that at my age, after so many years abroad, one could get so dreadfully homesick. What was in itself a wonderful motor expedition this morning . . . in the country . . . became almost unbearable . . . I thought how usefully I could be spending these hours in Germany. . . . I was in utter despair.[6]

Within days, he was on his way back home. While thousands were fleeing the coming war, Bonhoeffer sailed straight into the storm. Despite all the efforts to keep him out of harm's way, he returned to Germany—on the *Queen Mary*, the last steamer to cross the Atlantic before the outbreak of World War II.

TWENTY-THREE
FROM CLERGYMAN TO COURIER

1939–40

Dohnanyi was waiting with more secret documents for Bonhoeffer when he arrived home. He had proof of new atrocities. A group of Polish Jews had been herded into a cemetery and shot. Children with birth defects, the blind, the deaf, and the elderly were being sent to medical centers in the countryside, where they were murdered. Poles were declared *untermenschen* (subhuman) and enslaved in work camps.

It would not be enough to overthrow Hitler, Dohnanyi said. He had to be killed.

But what would happen to their souls if they were to commit murder? Dohnanyi asked. What about the Bible passage that said "all who take up the sword will perish by the sword"? (Matthew 26:52)

Hitler's brand of evil had "thrown all ethical concepts into confusion,"[1] Bonhoeffer told his brother-in-law and the other conspirators. "To think and to act with an eye on the coming generation and to be ready to move on without fear and worry—that is the course that has, in practice, been forced upon us."[2] With these words Bonhoeffer gave the conspirators the moral justification— and "the greatness of heart"[3]—to commit murder. He also offered them reassurance: "God promises forgiveness and consolation to a man who becomes a sinner in [such a] bold venture."[4]

As for himself, he said, "If I see a madman driving a car into a group of innocent bystanders, then I can't, as a Christian, simply wait for the catastrophe and then comfort the wounded and bury the dead. I must try and wrestle the steering wheel out of the hands of the driver."[5]

But how could a small group of conspirators get close enough to the Führer to kill him? Hitler's personal security was tight. All of his food was made by a private chef, then tested by his doctor. He wore a hat lined with steel. And his personal airplane cabin was armor-plated and outfitted with a parachute.

By now, a handful of military officers who knew about Hitler's crimes had joined the conspiracy. General Hans Oster and Admiral Wilhelm Canaris would play key roles in the plot, but the conspirators would need to find officers who could get close enough to Hitler to carry out their plan. A chance meeting between

Bonhoeffer and a German aristocrat would prove crucial in securing that help. But that wouldn't take place for some time to come.

Meanwhile, the conspirators needed a go-between with the outside world. Otherwise, they feared, Britain and France would take advantage of Hitler's death to attack Germany—and many more lives would be lost. And once Hitler was gone, the conspirators would need to show the Allies that there were "good Germans" they could deal with.

They needed someone who could travel back and forth to London inconspicuously. They needed someone who had a secret contact inside the British government. Was Dietrich Bonhoeffer willing to be that person?

THE OUTBREAK OF WORLD WAR II

- September 1, 1939—Germany invades Poland.
- September 3, 1939—Great Britain and France declare war on Germany. World War II officially begins.
- September 27, 1939—Poland surrenders.

By now, Dohnanyi was working for the Abwehr, a German intelligence agency, a job that gave him access to secret information about what was going on inside the government. His supervisor, Admiral Canaris, was also a member of the resistance and gave Dohnanyi free rein to continue collecting evidence of atrocities. He allowed Dohnanyi to hire Bonhoeffer as a counterintelligence officer. Not only would this permit Bonhoeffer to avoid the draft, he would now have a cover story for his travel outside of Germany. As far as anyone else could tell he would be collecting information valuable to the German government. But his real purpose was to smuggle damaging information out of the country, to tell foreign contacts about Hitler's atrocities, and to enlist their help in the coup. While traveling abroad he would also be in a perfect position to overhear information about military plans and pass it on to the conspirators.

Dietrich Bonhoeffer had wanted to use the moral authority of the church to fight Hitler. But by the time he returned from the United States, he was thoroughly disillusioned by the cowardice of his fellow clergy. Now he had a decision to make. To do nothing against Hitler was a sin, he had reasoned. But to kill was also a sin. How could a pacifist, a man of God, justify what he was about to do? The answer was one that had first been articulated by Martin Luther, the founder of the church Bonhoeffer had loved. Sometimes, Luther said, a true believer must "sin and sin boldly." Bonhoeffer would break the Commandments he had vowed to uphold and renounce his cherished philosophy of nonviolence. He would lie, cheat, and plot murder. And he would do it by using the church as his camouflage.

He would have to keep his role secret—from his friends and even other family members. And he would have to bide his time until he had a way to safely travel to London.

EVENTS OF 1940

- **May**—Germany attacks Holland, Belgium, Luxembourg, and France.
- **June**—The French surrender.

On June 19, 1940, Dietrich Bonhoeffer was sitting at an outdoor café with his friend Eberhard Bethge, enjoying the sunshine. They had tried to put recent events out of their minds, but it was impossible. Austria, Czechoslovakia, and Poland had already fallen to the Nazis. Holland and Belgium had fallen. Now German tanks were rolling across France.

When news came over the radio that France had surrendered, the café erupted in celebration. People jumped onto their chairs and began singing patriotic songs. People poured into the town square to cheer. The German public, so beaten down after World War I, was triumphant.

To Bethge's utter astonishment, Bonhoeffer leaped to his feet and gave the "Heil, Hitler!" salute.

Bonhoeffer couldn't tell his friend what he was doing, but Bethge would understand eventually. If his role in the conspiracy was to go unnoticed, Bonhoeffer would have to pretend he was loyal to Adolf Hitler.

The young pastor had become a double agent.

TWENTY-FOUR

UNDERCOVER

1940–41

Gusts of snow battered the windows of the ancient monastery where Bonhoeffer had holed up for a few months to work on a new book—and wait for his first assignment. Finally, he got word from Dohnanyi. He was being sent to Switzerland, ostensibly to gather intelligence for the Abwehr. In reality, he was meeting with Protestant church leaders from France and the Netherlands and presenting them with evidence of the latest atrocities in Germany and Poland.

Due to the Malicious Practices Act, very little of this information had escaped Germany. Surely, Bonhoeffer thought, once the rest of the world heard about Hitler's barbarity, their leaders would help the conspirators.

EVENTS OF 1941

- **April**—Germany conquers Yugoslavia, Greece, Albania, North Africa.
- **June**—Hitler invades Russia.

Undercover as a pastor, Bonhoeffer met with Archbishop Bell's contacts, in the hopes that Winston Churchill, the new prime minister of England, would be sympathetic to their cause. Many in the British government held the view that all Germans were Nazis, but Bonhoeffer had gone to Switzerland to show the world that there were good Germans willing to stand up to Hitler.

Bonhoeffer spelled out the Nazi atrocities and said there were Germans ready to risk their lives to overthrow Hitler—if only they could get support from Great Britain. Then he waited in vain for a reply. After a few weeks, he had to return home or risk blowing his cover.

But he went back again, this time taking an even more dangerous step.

Bell had sent word that Churchill wasn't interested in helping the conspirators; he wasn't even convinced a conspiracy existed. And so Bonhoeffer wrote a memo that described the conspiracy in detail. Later, at a private meeting with Bell in Sweden, he even named some of the prominent members of the group. He tried desperately to prove that the resistance had real support in the military and that they would succeed. This information, if it fell into the wrong hands, would mean execution for all those involved.

"You can rely on it," Bonhoeffer said. "We shall overthrow Hitler!"[1]

Still, the British were unwilling to help. Unbeknownst to Bonhoeffer, Churchill wanted a complete military victory over Hitler, nothing less. His foreign secretary dismissed Bonhoeffer in a letter where he wrote, "I see no reason whatsoever to encourage this pestilent priest."[2]

But Bonhoeffer didn't give up. He asked Archbishop Bell to pass his memo on to the American ambassador. He never heard back.

During one of his trips to Switzerland, Bonhoeffer went to visit his former mentor, the theologian Karl Barth. "Why are you actually here?" Barth asked. When Bonhoeffer told him he had joined the conspiracy, Barth was angry. How could a pacifist join such a violent movement? he asked. How could a pastor justify being involved in a plot to kill the leader of his government while other young German men were giving their lives on the front lines of a war? And how could such a crazy scheme succeed?

Bonhoeffer returned home, dispirited, to the streets of Berlin, where Jews were now forced to wear yellow stars pinned to their clothing. "If you want to know the truth," he wrote to a friend, "I pray for the defeat of my nation. For I believe it is the only way to pay for all the suffering which my country has caused in the world."[3] He not only prayed for Germany's defeat, he prayed for Hitler's death—and he prayed with the men who had pledged to carry it out.

One night at Dohnanyi's house, he said, if necessary, *he* would kill Hitler.

His brother-in-law said the plotters needed him more as their spiritual leader. And he said they had another assignment for him.

Operation 7 was the code name for a plan to help seven Jews, including a woman named Charlotte Friedenthal, escape the country. Even though she'd been baptized at birth, Friedenthal was forced to wear a yellow Star of David on her coat because she had "Jewish blood." All her relatives had fled the country, but she had remained, devoted to her work for the Confessing Church. Now that the little breakaway church had been ruled illegal, she, too, needed to flee. Bonhoeffer tried to intercede for her and six others with the Swiss.

But they were unwilling to help. Bonhoeffer explained that Dohnanyi had gotten Friedenthal and the six others forged documents letters of safe passage to Switzerland. But still the Swiss refused.

Finally, Dohnanyi broke the impasse: He would transfer a large amount of currency to a Swiss bank to pay the refugees' expenses once they arrived. It was a violation of wartime currency restrictions, but it had to be done. Bonhoeffer, meanwhile, went to his church contacts in Switzerland and arranged for visas and sponsors for the group—which had now grown from seven people to fourteen. Friedenthal was the first to leave; the others arrived safely in Basel a few weeks later. Operation 7 was a success—but it would prove to be Dohnanyi's and Bonhoeffer's undoing.

TWENTY-FIVE
SOUNDING THE ALARM

1941

On October 5, 1941, Jews in Berlin began receiving letters telling them their homes had been scheduled for what was being called an "evacuation." On the night of October 16, they were taken from their homes and gathered at a local synagogue for deportation. One of the people who received such a notice was a sixty-year-old woman who had been a longtime friend of the Bonhoeffer family. She was told to leave her home and report to a nearby train station. There, she was herded, along with hundreds of others, onto a cattle car.

EVENTS OF 1941

- **September**—Jews are required to wear a yellow Star of David on their clothing.
- **October**—Bonhoeffer is the first to report the mass evacuations of Jews from Berlin, Cologne, and other cities.
- **December**—Japan attacks Pearl Harbor. The United States enters the war.

As soon as he heard this, Bonhoeffer set to work gathering information. He found that some 1,600 Jews had been rounded up and deported by train from Berlin, some at a train station just a mile from his house. Jews who worked at the Siemens munitions plant were taken straight from the factory floor to the transit depots. In just three weeks, sixty thousand Jews had vanished from Berlin.

"Exact numbers are not known at this point,"[1] Bonhoeffer wrote in a report to his coconspirators. But as more and more notices went out to Jewish families, he said, they knew what was in store for them. "The despair is unprecedented."[2] He also included information about mass deportations from elsewhere in Germany: Jews from Cologne, Düsseldorf, and Elberfeld were being sent to Poland.

A few days later, he added to his report, warning that

more deportations were scheduled for the nights of October 23 and 28. Soon, flyers began going up in neighborhoods near the Bonhoeffer home: "Every German who in any way supports a Jew . . . even through friendly encounter, commits a betrayal of our people."[3]

Sick with pneumonia, Bonhoeffer stayed up through the night, working on documentation for Dohnanyi to pass on to the conspirators in the military. He also found a way to sneak a copy of the report out of the country, to one of his contacts in Geneva. It was high treason. It was written proof of Hitler's plans to rid the country of non-Aryans. And, according to the Berlin State Library, where the original letter is kept, it was the first time anyone had told the outside world what was happening to the Jews of Germany.

A young man, writing from a small, cramped study in his parents' home, was likely the first to ring the alarm about what would become the Holocaust, a genocide that would kill six million men, women, and children. Reports of the systematic deportation of Jews would not appear in the press for another year. By then, it would be too late for millions of people.

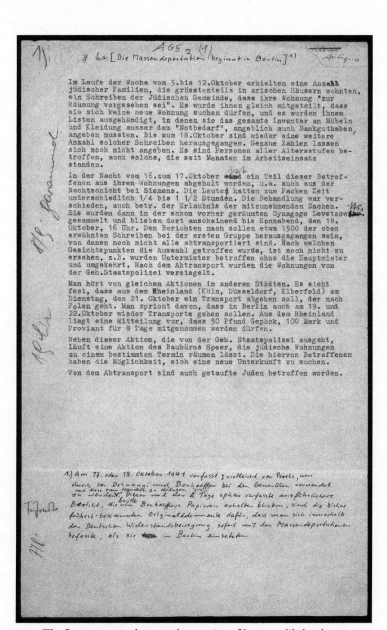

[handwritten at top] A G5 2 (1)

[handwritten] 8 bef. [Die Massendeportation beginnt in Berlin] ¹⁾

Im Laufe der Woche vom 5.bis 12.Oktober erhielten eine Anzahl
jüdischer Familien, die grösstenteils in arischen Häusern wohnten,
ein Schreiben der Jüdischen Gemeinde, dass ihre Wohnung "zur
Räumung vorgesehen sei". Es wurde ihnen gleich mitgeteilt, dass
sie sich keine neue Wohnung suchen dürfen, und es wurden ihnen
Listen ausgehändigt, in denen sie das gesamte Inventar an Möbeln
und Kleidung ausser dem "Notbedarf", angeblich auch Bankguthaben,
angeben mussten. Bis zum 18.Oktober sind wieder eine weitere
Anzahl solcher Schreiben herausgegangen. Genaue Zahlen lassen
sich noch nicht angeben. Es sind Personen aller Altersstufen betroffen, auch solche, die seit Monaten im Arbeitseinsatz
standen.

In der Nacht vom 16.zum 17.Oktober sind ein Teil dieser Betroffenen aus ihren Wohnungen abgeholt worden, u.a. auch aus der
Nachtschicht bei Siemens. Die Leute hatten zum Packen Zeit
unterschiedlich 1/4 bis 1 1/2 Stunden. Die Behandlung war ver-
schieden, auch betr. der Erlaubnis der mitzunehmenden Sachen.
Sie wurden dann in der schon vorher geräumten Synagoge Levetzow-
gesammelt und blieben dort anscheinend bis Sonnabend, den 18.
Oktober, 16 Uhr. Den Berichten nach sollen etwa 1500 der oben
erwähnten Schreiben bei der ersten Gruppe herausgegangen sein,
von denen noch nicht alle abtransportiert sind. Nach welchen
Gesichtspunkten die Auswahl getroffen wurde, ist noch nicht zu
ersehen, z.B. wurden Untermieter betroffen ohne die Hauptmieter
und umgekehrt. Nach dem Abtransport wurden die Wohnungen von
der Geh.Staatspolizei versiegelt.

Man hört von gleichen Aktionen in anderen Städten. Es steht
fest, dass aus dem Rheinland (Köln, Düsseldorf, Elberfeld) am
Dienstag, den 21. Oktober ein Transport abgehen soll, der nach
Polen geht. Man spricht davon, dass in Berlin auch am 19. und
22.Oktober wieder Transporte gehen sollen. Aus dem Rheinland
liegt eine Mitteilung vor, dass 50 Pfund Gepäck, 100 Mark und
Proviant für 8 Tage mitgenommen werden dürfen.

Neben dieser Aktion, die von der Geh. Staatspolizei ausgeht,
läuft eine Aktion des Baubüros Speer, die jüdische Wohnungen
zu einem bestimmten Termin räumen lässt. Die hiervon Betroffenen
haben die Möglichkeit, sich eine neue Unterkunft zu suchen.

Von dem Abtransport sind auch getaufte Juden betroffen worden.

[handwritten footnote] 1.) Am 17. oder 18. Oktober 1941 verfasst (vielleicht von Perels, um
durch von Dohnanyi und Bonhoeffer bei den Generälen verwendet
und diese zum Handeln zu drängen)
zu werden. Dieser und der 2 Tage später verfasste ausführlichere
Bericht, die beide Bonhoeffers Papieren erhalten blieben, sind die bisher
frühest-bekannten Originaldokumente dafür, dass man sich innerhalb
der Deutschen Widerstandsbewegung sofort mit den Massendeportationen
befasste, als sie in Berlin einsetzten.

The first report on the mass deportation of Jews was likely a letter
written by Dietrich Bonhoeffer, dated October 18, 1941

THE FINAL SOLUTION

Bonhoeffer wrote his report in October 1941. In early 1942, Hitler's men met at a villa in Wannsee to further refine a plan in which Europe would be "combed through from west to east for Jews."[4] But the Nazis were too careful to spell out their plans for the extermination of all eleven million men, women, and children in Europe. Instead, they said Jews would be "eliminated by natural causes"[5]—coded language for starvation and hard labor. It would be, they decreed, the "Final Solution." In 1942 alone, more than 4.5 million people would be killed in concentration camps. It was one of the "most astounding years of murder in the whole history of mankind," according to historian Mark Roseman.[6]

TWENTY-SIX
LOVE IN WARTIME

1942

On April 10, 1942, a dense, soupy fog shrouded the coast of Norway as Bonhoeffer paced the ferry terminal. It was his third trip out of the country as a double agent. He had come to Norway a few days earlier, ostensibly on a mission for the Abwehr; in reality, he was there to meet with foreign officials and convince them that the plot to assassinate Hitler was real. Bonhoeffer was eager to get home and report to the conspirators, but the fog meant that no boats would be leaving that day.

The delay, however, would prove fateful. Helmuth James Graf von Moltke, a wealthy German landowner and military man, was also stranded at the same ferry terminal. Moltke had already expressed misgivings about what he saw in the streets of Berlin. Every day, he said, "Jews are being rounded up. Then they are sent off with what they can carry. . . . How can anyone know these things and walk around free?" He grappled with his conscience, wondering, "What shall I say when I am asked: And what did you do during that time?"[1]

But Moltke, like many in the aristocracy, was morally opposed to assassinating Hitler. He was more interested in preparing for a democratic Germany after Hitler fell. As they waited for the fog to lift, the two men took a long walk on the beach to the chalky cliffs of a nearby town. Moltke said he objected to a violent removal of Hitler; Bonhoeffer, the former pacifist, argued that the conspirators needed to take up arms. God would forgive them.

After the weather broke and the two men sailed home, Moltke brought Bonhoeffer's words to a gathering of military and civilian leaders at his country estate in Kreisau a few weeks later. It was at that meeting that the Kreisau Circle was formed. The members of this group found the soldiers who would carry out the assassination attempt.

EVENTS OF 1942

- **January**—The Final Solution for the extermination of the Jews is adopted.
- **May**—The British begin bombing Germany.
- **June**—Bonhoeffer meets Maria von Wedemeyer.

THE KREISAU CIRCLE

There were several resistance groups in existence in Germany by 1942. Each cell operated underground, often without contact or awareness of the others. The Kreisau Circle was a group of aristocrats mostly interested in forming a government after the fall of the Nazis. The Oster-Canaris ring was a group of military men who, after witnessing some of Hitler's atrocities, vowed to take up arms against him. Hans Oster was an army general in charge of counterespionage at the Abwehr; he and Wilhelm Canaris, an admiral who led the Abwehr, gave Dohnanyi the freedom to collect evidence against the Nazis and to hire Bonhoeffer as a spy.

When Bonhoeffer returned from Norway, his brother and brothers-in-law were waiting for him at their parents' home. They didn't say much, but invited Dietrich to sit down at the piano and play a few songs. The whole family, including the wives and children, gathered around the piano and sang. Meanwhile, Dohnanyi leaned over and whispered in Dietrich's ear. He had bad news: The Gestapo was watching Dietrich. Dohnanyi's own phone had been tapped and his letters were being intercepted.

Bonhoeffer drew up a will and gave it to his friend Eberhard Bethge; he didn't want to alarm his parents. But the conspirators would use these family musical evenings for some time to come—as cover for their meetings.

Back in Berlin, Dietrich Bonhoeffer strolled beneath the linden trees, smoking cigarettes. He put on his tuxedo and went to the opera. He went to the ballet, to the movies, and out to dinner with friends. He had even managed to visit his favorite haberdashery when he was in Geneva.

Meanwhile, friends began to wonder: How was he able to travel to Switzerland, England, and Norway during wartime? How was he able to enjoy himself while his former students had been drafted and were fighting and dying? What had happened to Dietrich Bonhoeffer, the firebrand pastor? He was working for the Abwehr. Had he sold out to the Nazis?

Bonhoeffer could confide in no one, not even his closest friends. He wasn't free to write about this agony in his diary, for fear it would fall into the wrong hands. In fact, he kept up a steady stream of letters to Sabine with bland and cheerful descriptions of his travels and writings. He couldn't even tell his twin sister how he really felt.

In the middle of this lonely and dangerous time, Bonhoeffer fell in love.

He had gone back to the Pomeranian hills to continue his writing and to see an old friend who had supported the seminary of the Confessing Church when it was in existence nearby. While he was at the home of Ruth von Kleist-Retzow, her eighteen-year-old granddaughter arrived for a visit. Could this be the little girl Bonhoeffer had taught in confirmation class years ago? Pretty and vivacious, Maria von Wedemeyer was confident, sunny—and opinionated. She told Bonhoeffer she read his book before bed at night—but said she could barely finish a sentence before falling asleep!

Her passion for life was contagious. And it was just what the disheartened young theologian needed. He was smitten.

Because of their age difference—Dietrich was thirty-six and Maria was eighteen—her mother didn't approve of the two marrying right away. Besides, it was wartime, her mother said, and the future was uncertain. They should wait a year. And so the two wrote letters to each other almost every day.

What no one knew was that the Gestapo had already found an accounting entry relating to the smuggling of currency to Switzerland for Operation 7. They interrogated an Abwehr employee who gave them three names: Hans von Dohnanyi, Hans Oster (one of Dohnanyi's superiors at the Abwehr), and Dietrich Bonhoeffer. The conspirators didn't know it yet, but they were running out of time.

TWENTY-SEVEN
THE NOOSE GROWS TIGHTER

1942

Servants were removing the dinner dishes and serving coffee at a country parsonage where Bonhoeffer was visiting a friend. One of the dinner guests, a young staff lieutenant in the army high command, had been oddly silent all night. Now, he turned to Bonhoeffer and asked a question.

"Shall I shoot?" he said. "I can get inside the Führer's headquarters with my revolver."[1]

EVENTS OF NOVEMBER 1942

• Hitler's troops suffer defeats in Russia.

• British troops defeat German army in North Africa.

It was November 1942, and the conspiracy was at a low point. Here was a young man, Werner von Haeften, offering to undertake the most dangerous mission imaginable. The conspirators had been gathering evidence against Hitler and plotting to kill him now for two years. They were playing a dangerous cat-and-mouse game with the Gestapo, their every move monitored, their mail opened, their phones tapped. They spoke in code because they knew that Nazi spies were everywhere. This hotheaded young man could bring the conspiracy crashing down and send Bonhoeffer and the others to their deaths.

Bonhoeffer tried to dissuade him. Any attempt on Hitler's life had to be well planned, and the conspirators needed to have new leadership in place ready to run the country. An unplanned assassination might only make things worse, or it could turn Hitler into a martyr. And surely Haeften would die in the attempt.

But the young officer wouldn't be pacified. What does one life matter compared to all those who might be saved by getting rid of the madman? he asked Bonhoeffer. So, he said, "Shall I shoot?"

Bonhoeffer said he couldn't make the decision for him. He simply said what he had told Dohnanyi and Moltke. No one would emerge from Hitler's reign without guilt—those who did nothing or those who took action.

Haeften returned to his military duties. Later, he would play a key role in an attempt on Hitler's life.

Meanwhile, Bonhoeffer kept up his dangerous overseas trips as a spy and courier. He snuck into Italy, Switzerland, and Sweden, pleading for help from his contacts there. By now Dohnanyi's Chronicle of Shame included more evidence: films of concentration camp atrocities in Poland, a copy of the instructions for the campaign against the Jews. Surely, Bonhoeffer thought, this would be enough to open the eyes of the world to Hitler's cruelty. Each time he traveled abroad, the Gestapo kept an eye on him. And each time, his pleas for help were met with complete silence.

It was his faith in the righteousness of their mission that kept Bonhoeffer from total despair. "I am hopeful that the day might not be too far when the bad dream will be over and we shall meet again,"[2] he wrote to Sabine. It was the last letter she would receive from her brother as a free man.

Meanwhile, the noose was tightening. Bonhoeffer knew he was being followed; he had even heard a rumor that he was going to be arrested any day. And so he began to keep a bogus diary about his travels—to confuse and mislead the Gestapo.

The fake diary was filled with boring descriptions about the weather and the sights in the towns he visited. He also slipped in little messages he hoped the Nazis would see. He called an especially dull Nazi official "a very . . . smart old world officer," and described another officer, a well-known bore, as a "bon vivant."[3]

Whenever he went out, he left the diary open on his desk—in case the Gestapo searched his parents' home. A few months later, when the two Nazi officials came to his study, it was lying there.

TWENTY-EIGHT
ASSASSINATION ATTEMPTS

1943

One night in March 1943, Hans von Dohnanyi asked if he could borrow his father-in-law's car. The car had a special permit, available only to doctors, that allowed it to be driven at night. Dohnanyi raced to catch a train to the German border, where Hitler was visiting to survey the war effort. Inside Dohnanyi's suitcase was a special fuse, a silent detonator that he would deliver to another member of the conspiracy.

With the Gestapo on their trail, the plotters had decided the time had come to act—whether they had the support of the Allies or not. They would assassinate Hitler now—and then send Bonhoeffer to ask foreign governments to work peacefully with the new German leadership.

By this time, the resistance had grown to include several high-ranking military men. One of them, Fabian von Schlabrendorff, was waiting for the arrival of the fuse. He would rig it to a bomb disguised as a bottle of cognac, and the next day he would sneak the "cognac" onto Hitler's plane. After the bomb exploded and Hitler's plane went down, generals connected to the plotters would stage a coup.

Dohnanyi hurried back home and waited. By midday, he got word that the bomb had been placed in the plane's cargo hold. Dohnanyi, Bonhoeffer, and his parents sat by the radio and waited for the news of the explosion. But two hours later, they heard the unbelievable: The bomb had failed to go off. The conspirators were devastated—but relieved that they hadn't been discovered. And they quickly came up with another plan— which they executed just a few days later.

This time they used two bombs, not one, strapped inside the overcoat of a conspirator in the military, an army officer named Major Rudolph-Christoph von Gersdorff. Hitler was coming to Gersdorff's barracks to review some captured weaponry; when he arrived Gersdorff would break a tiny vial of acid that would light the fuse. It would take ten minutes for the bomb to go off; Gersdorff would die in the effort.

The Bonhoeffer family was gathered around the piano at home on March 21, 1943, practicing a song that they planned to sing at their father's seventy-fifth birthday party. Dietrich was at the keyboard; Ursula's husband, Rüdiger Schleicher, also a member of the conspiracy, played the violin. As they all sang, Hans von Dohnanyi and Klaus Bonhoeffer kept their eyes on the clock. The bomb would go off—just six miles away—at any minute.

They waited for the phone to ring. Finally, Gersdorff sent word. He'd hit the button releasing the acid as soon as Hitler had arrived; the acid was eating its way toward the fuse when the Führer unexpectedly left! Gersdorff ran into a restroom and tore the bomb apart. Hitler had escaped again.

Gersdorff was never caught. But there was bad news from Dohnanyi's sources a few days later: Hitler's men were onto the conspirators.

TWENTY-NINE

CAUGHT

1943—44

On April 5, 1943, when Bonhoeffer called Dohnanyi's home, a strange voice answered the phone. Bonhoeffer hung up. He knew then that the Gestapo had finally caught up with them. They were searching Dohnanyi's house right that very minute. His parents' house would be next.

Calmly he went next door, where his sister Ursula lived. He told her the Gestapo would soon arrive and arrest him. She made him a hearty lunch. It was the last home-cooked meal he would ever have.

Meanwhile, Hans von Dohnanyi was being arrested, along with his wife, Dietrich's sister Christel.

Bonhoeffer's fiancée, Maria von Wedemeyer, far away in the

countryside, wrote in her diary that day, describing a terrible feeling of dread. "Has something bad happened?" she wrote. "I'm afraid it's something very bad."[1]

When a black SS Mercedes pulled up outside his parents' home, Bonhoeffer was ready. He had opened his diary to a page with a handful of fake entries and hidden his important papers in a secret panel in the attic. His papers would remain there, untouched, for years. He kissed his parents good-bye and left with the two Gestapo agents, his brother Walter's Bible in his hand.

The next morning, a heel of bread was thrown into Bonhoeffer's small, dirty cell at Tegel prison. He had to pick it up from the floor to eat it. In the cell next to his, a man was weeping. As Bonhoeffer's eyes grew used to the dim light, he saw some graffiti on the wall, evidently written by someone who'd been held there before him. "In a hundred years," it said, "it'll all be over."[2]

For the next twelve days, Bonhoeffer was shackled hand and foot. There was nothing in his cell except a wooden bed, a stool, and a bucket. The door to his cell opened once a day, to bring the food in and the slop out.

His captors soon realized that Dietrich Bonhoeffer was from a prominent family—indeed, the warden was his uncle. Meanwhile, Bonhoeffer had won over the guards with his good behavior. And so they allowed his family to send him small gifts—slippers, shaving cream, writing paper, ink, and tobacco.

He and Maria kept up their correspondence, although Bonhoeffer had not told her about his role in the conspiracy as a way of protecting her. He also wrote to his parents. "I do want you to be quite sure that I'm all right. . . . Strangely enough, the discomforts one associates with prison life, the physical hardships, hardly bother me at all."[3]

He was also allowed to receive books: books with infinitesimally small pencil marks under a letter every ten pages or so. It was a code—prearranged before the arrest—that allowed Bonhoeffer and Dohnanyi to keep their stories straight when they were being interrogated by their jailers.

Bonhoeffer's mother also sent her son homemade jam in a jar with a secret double lid. He and Dohnanyi communicated by hiding letters—in tiny script—in between the two thin pieces of cardboard in the lid.

EVENTS OF 1943–44

- July 1943—Allied troops land in Sicily.
- September 1943—Allied troops land in Naples.
- December 1943—Soviet troops defeat German troops in Kiev.
- June 1944—Allied troops land in Normandy, open a second front against Germany.
- August 1944—Paris is liberated; Allied troops arrive at German border.

The Nazis, however, were completely unaware of Bonhoeffer's involvement in the assassination conspiracy. He had been jailed for sending money out of the country as part of Operation 7. The Nazis, it seemed, couldn't imagine that the pastor on staff with the Abwehr would be disloyal. They couldn't imagine that members of the German intelligence agency were helping Jews escape. They thought the transfer of German currency to Switzerland was some kind of money-laundering scheme—a greedy act, perhaps, but not a treasonous one.

Dohnanyi was interrogated relentlessly—about the monetary discrepancies, about Bonhoeffer's travels—but as soon as he realized the Nazis were unaware of his involvement in the assassination attempts, he was able to breathe a little more easily. He sent Bonhoeffer coded messages inside a book, telling him the good news. And so Dohnanyi and Bonhoeffer and the others continued their planning for the next assassination attempt—right under the noses of the Nazis.

Meanwhile, Hitler's army was on the run in Russia. And Allied planes buzzed over Berlin night and day, dropping deadly bombs nearby. The prison windows shattered and the ground quaked. As they knelt amid broken glass, waiting to die, Bonhoeffer ministered to his fellow prisoners—and guards. During quiet spells, he continued working on his book or writing to Maria. He would be in prison for almost two years.

Bonhoeffer was interrogated, but his star status as the warden's nephew meant that he was never tortured or subjected to the brutal questioning that Dohnanyi endured. When the Gestapo questioned him, he pretended to be a simple pastor, unfamiliar with the workings of the Abwehr. But he never gave up his belief that all his actions in the resistance were morally justified. "The thing for which I should be condemned is so irreproachable that I may only be proud of it,"[4] he wrote.

No matter how uncomfortable the conditions, Bonhoeffer had his own way of escaping: He would lie on his plank bed and dream of lying under the rose arbor at his childhood home. "In my imagination," he said, "I lie on my back in the grass, watch the clouds sailing in the breeze across the blue sky, and listen to the rustle of the leaves."[5]

One day, Bonhoeffer's uncle showed up at his cell with several bottles of champagne. The celebration could only mean one thing: The war would soon be over. Bonhoeffer was so certain that he'd be released at any minute that he wrote to Maria to tell her to go ahead with their wedding planning. "Our marriage," he wrote to his fiancée, "must be a 'yes' to God's earth."[6]

THIRTY
ANOTHER ATTEMPT ON HITLER'S LIFE

1944

On July 20, 1944, two officers pulled up at the security check-point for a meeting at Hitler's bunker at the Wolf's Lair, his heavily guarded compound near Russia on the eastern front of the war. One of them, a young lieutenant colonel named Claus Schenk Graf von Stauffenberg, held a briefcase by his side. The other was his aide, Werner von Haeften, the young man who'd asked Bonhoeffer, "Shall I shoot?"

Stauffenberg entered the map room with his briefcase. Inside it was a bomb. Just before Hitler was due to arrive, he slipped into a private room. He pulled out a pair of special pliers, adapted so that Stauffenberg, who had lost his right hand in combat, could arm the bomb. A guard knocked on the door, telling him to hurry, the meeting was starting any minute. Stauffenberg returned to the conference room and put the briefcase under the map table—just six feet from Hitler's leg.

With just three minutes before the bomb would go off, Stauffenberg excused himself. He walked out of the building, toward his waiting car, fighting the urge to break into a run. He and Haeften bluffed their way past the checkpoint and drove away. Moments later, the bunker erupted in flames.

When the smoke cleared, the heavy oak map table was in splinters and several people were dead. But Hitler was alive. His hair stood on end and his pants were in tatters. But he was giddy with relief. He went on the radio almost immediately to let the German people know that their leader was fine. "I see this as another sign from Providence that I must and therefore shall continue my work,"[1] he said.

Stauffenberg and Haeften were caught and executed by firing squad a little after midnight the next day.

Bonhoeffer was in the sick bay ministering to a fellow prisoner when he heard the Führer's triumphant voice on the radio. He was crestfallen. Then he got word that the Gestapo had gone on a massive raid, rounding up anyone they thought was connected to the conspiracy. They found letters, diaries, and documents that led to even more arrests. But Dohnanyi's

Chronicle of Shame, safely stored in a crate in a suburb of Berlin, was untouched.

Then they got word that Admiral Canaris, a key member of the conspiracy, had been arrested.

THIRTY-ONE
EVIDENCE OF TREASON

1944

By now, some of the conspirators had moved Dohnanyi's secret files to another hiding place, in a cellar at a hunting lodge in the country. But a few items were left behind at the military base outside Berlin, and someone tipped off the Nazis that there was information there that they might find interesting.

On September 20, a search party found the rest of Dohnanyi's Chronicle of Shame. Inside the crate were documents that tied him directly to the July 20 bombing. And inside one file were three handwritten notes from Bonhoeffer, notes that implicated him as an Abwehr spy.

Hans von Dohnanyi wrote a coded letter to his wife,

Christel: "I don't know who the traitor is. Ultimately, it doesn't matter to me, but they have everything."[1] Soon, he was sent to the Sachsenhausen concentration camp.

Bonhoeffer knew it was only a matter of time before he would be tied to the conspirators. He wrote to his old friend Eberhard Bethge that day, including a poem that said, "Death / Come now, thou greatest of feasts on the journey to freedom eternal."[2] The eternity he'd been imagining since those long ago nights in his childhood bedroom seemed to be at hand.

Maria came to see him the day after Dohnanyi was transferred to the Sachsenhausen concentration camp. She had begun to suffer headaches, insomnia, and fainting spells, but on that day, Bonhoeffer would write, she was "steadfast . . . in a way I've rarely seen."[3] It was the last time they would ever see each other.

Now the days became grim. The Gestapo threatened to go after his parents—or even Maria—if he didn't divulge what he knew about the conspiracy. And Bonhoeffer, despite his faith, suffered doubts about his ability to sustain much more. He even considered suicide, "not from a sense of guilt," he wrote, "but because I am basically already dead."[4]

But one of the guards who had grown fond of Bonhoeffer had a plan. A guard named Knoblauch had gotten a mechanic's uniform in Bonhoeffer's size and sneaked it into the prison. He had also hidden food coupons and money in a garden shed near the prison. When the time was right, he told Bonhoeffer, all he had to do was slip on the uniform and simply walk out with Knoblauch at the end of his shift. After his escape, he could go to the garden shed and get the supplies he needed to flee the country.

Then Bonhoeffer got word that the Gestapo had arrested his brother Klaus. Soon, his brother-in-law Rüdiger Schleicher would be taken. Now, the four men—two brothers and two brothers-in-law—who had been gathered around the piano at the Bonhoeffer home were all imprisoned.

A few days after Klaus's arrest, Colonel Knoblauch knocked on the door to the Bonhoeffer home. Dietrich Bonhoeffer had decided not to escape, he told them; it would only make things worse for everyone, especially Klaus and Rudy.

On October 8, 1944, Bonhoeffer was led from his prison cell to a courtyard outside. It was the first time he'd seen the sunlight in eighteen months. He was taken to an underground Gestapo prison in Berlin. Before he got into the van that would take him away, his brother Walter's Bible, the one he had carried with him everywhere since he was fifteen, was taken from his hands.

It was not until their parcels and letters were sent back to them that Bonhoeffer's family and fiancée realized he was no longer at Tegel prison.

Dietrich Bonhoeffer in the yard of Tegel prison in Berlin, July 1944

THIRTY-TWO
THE END OF THE WAR

1945

On February 3, 1945, the skies over Berlin darkened as nearly one thousand Allied Flying Fortress bombers roared overhead, dropping three thousand tons of bombs.

Some of the bombs hit the Gestapo prison where Bonhoeffer was being held. And some landed on the court where, just the day before, Klaus Bonhoeffer and Rüdiger Schleicher had been sentenced to death.

The war was coming to an end, and it would only be a matter of time until Germany was defeated. Bonhoeffer prayed for the strength to hang on. Then, without warning, he was transferred to the Buchenwald concentration camp. Huddled in the cold with his fellow prisoners at Buchenwald, Bonhoeffer urged them to keep faith. At any moment, they might be liberated. Or they might find a way to escape.

What he didn't say was that at any minute they might also be killed. Even as the Allies inched closer, the killings at Buchenwald continued. On April 1, Easter Sunday, the Allies got so close, the guards told the prisoners to get ready to leave.

Days passed. Then, with no explanation, Bonhoeffer was hauled out of his barracks and put in a van crowded full of prisoners. As he and the other inmates traveled through the Bavarian hillsides, Bonhoeffer shared his last small stash of tobacco. After traveling for hours, the van stopped and the doors opened.

Somehow, in the midst of war, spring had arrived. The prisoners, a dozen or so men and two women, climbed out of the van into an impossibly beautiful April day. They were standing in front of a picture-book farmhouse, where the farmer's wife brought them fresh rye bread and a jug of milk. After this small picnic, they climbed back in the van and continued on their way to a small town called Schönberg, where they would be temporarily held in a schoolhouse.

On Sunday, April 8, 1945, some of the prisoners asked Bonhoeffer to conduct a prayer service. In the whitewashed classroom where they were being held, he prayed and read to the prisoners as if he were teaching Sunday school back in Harlem—with a clear, patient, and comforting tone. Just as he finished the closing prayer, the door opened, and two men took him away. He would be dead the next day.

THIRTY-THREE
ETERNITY AT LAST

APRIL 1945

The stench of death filled the air even before the van reached Flossenbürg concentration camp. Initially a work camp where inmates quarried gravel for Hitler's building projects, such as the Autobahn, Flossenbürg now housed all kinds of "social aliens,"[1] such as gypsies, gays, vagabonds, dissidents, and Jews. It was surrounded by a tall wall with an electrified fence and six granite watchtowers; the SS flag, with its skull and crossbones insignia, flew overhead. A plaque greeted the new arrivals: "There is a path to freedom and its milestones are obedience, hard work, honesty, order, cleanliness, sobriety, truthfulness, a spirit of self-sacrifice and love of the Fatherland."[2]

The camp was rife with disease and overcrowded beyond

imagining. Barracks designed to hold 250 people now held a thousand, with inmates sleeping four to a bunk. The crematorium, where inmates were taken after they'd been worked or starved to death, had been operating so incessantly, it had temporarily broken down.

When Bonhoeffer arrived at Flossenbürg he was taken to a special barracks for political prisoners. A low, white building, it was divided into open stalls, where Bonhoeffer was held along with other inmates, including two other members of the conspiracy, Admiral Canaris and General Oster.

Bonhoeffer was only at Flossenbürg one day. The next morning, April 9, he, Canaris, Oster, and three other men were forced to undress and led to a gallows in a small courtyard right in front of their barracks. Before he was hanged, Bonhoeffer knelt and prayed. A doctor who observed the execution said, "I have never seen a man die so entirely submissive to the will of God."[3] As the noose was put around his neck, he whispered a prayer, completely calm and ready, at last, to meet eternity.

A little while later, Fabian von Schlabrendorff, the man who'd put the bomb on Hitler's plane, watched from a window in his cell as Bonhoeffer's body was carried away. His corpse was thrown on a giant bonfire and burned in the open.

Two weeks later, on April 23, the Allies marched into Flossenbürg. The camp was nearly deserted. Most of the SS officers had fled before their arrival, but the Allied soldiers found 1,600 desperately ill prisoners—and a stack of charred bones and decomposing bodies. They buried the remains in a mass grave at a cemetery in Flossenbürg and forced the local citizens to attend the ceremony.

There is no way to know if Bonhoeffer's body was cremated in the bonfire or if his remains are in that mass grave. There is no headstone to mark the grave of the boy who dreamed of eternity.

Flossenbürg concentration camp, ruins of the execution yard
where Dietrich Bonhoeffer was hanged on April 9, 1945

EPILOGUE

Hans von Dohnanyi was killed on April 8, 1945, on direct orders from Hitler.

Klaus Bonhoeffer and Rüdiger Schleicher were killed by a firing squad on April 23, the same day the Allies liberated Flossenbürg.

On April 30, Adolf Hitler committed suicide, taking a cyanide capsule, then shooting himself in the head.

The war in Europe ended on May 8, 1945.

Maria von Wedemeyer, Bonhoeffer's fiancée, traveled for two days, then walked seven kilometers to the camp at Flossenbürg, desperately seeking news about him. She was turned away with no information.

Back in Berlin, Bonhoeffer's parents got word about the

deaths of Dohnanyi, Schleicher, and their son Klaus. But they knew nothing about Dietrich. Months passed. Someone even claimed to have seen him alive. On July 27, they turned on the radio to hear the voice of Archbishop George Bell, Bonhoeffer's secret contact in London, giving a eulogy for a young pastor he'd met years earlier "as an emissary of the Resistance to Hitler."[1] This was how Dietrich Bonhoeffer's parents learned that their son was dead.

AUTHOR'S NOTE

All of us see injustice. In our schools, in our country, in the world. But very few of us speak out—especially if we ourselves aren't directly affected. And even fewer of us put our own lives at risk on behalf of others.

When I heard about a young minister involved in the conspiracy to kill Hitler, I could hardly believe it. What would make a quiet, scholarly pastor commit treason? What would make a pacifist sign on to an assassination plot? How could a man of faith justify murder?

Hans von Dohnanyi, the man who brought Bonhoeffer into the conspiracy, put it quite simply when he said that the members of the resistance were "on the path that a decent person inevitably takes."[1]

We all like to think that we would follow that path if we were confronted with injustice. But so few do. Dietrich Bonhoeffer had every opportunity to avoid it. Yet he committed himself, heart and soul, to a journey that would lead him to break the law and trespass against the commandments. Why? Because, as he put it, to do nothing "in the face of evil is evil itself."

Does the fact that he didn't succeed in his aims make him any less of a hero? Or does the fact that he died for his beliefs tell us something important about the nature of heroism?

There are no easy answers to these questions, but it is interesting to know that Bonhoeffer himself wrestled with them.

After his death, the secret writings that he had hidden in his parents' attic would be unearthed, and his prison writings would be published. Those words are just as relevant today, as they ask who among us will speak out. They are words that have inspired many acts of civil disobedience in the years since they were written.

His writings were translated into English and passed around jail cells in the South during the civil rights movement and read to discouraged protestors. Martin Luther King, Jr., seemed to echo Bonhoeffer's words when he said, "He who passively accepts evil is as much involved in it as he who helps perpetuate it."[2] Bonhoeffer's famous speech calling on people of good will to "jam a stick in the wheels of government"[3] was quoted by student demonstrators in the United States in the 1960s. And they were invoked by Archbishop Desmond Tutu in the campaign against apartheid in South Africa. All around the world, they have inspired those who risk their personal freedom to stand up for justice.

The letter Bonhoeffer hid in the attic the day the Nazis came to arrest him seems to ask a question of all of us even today:

> *We have been silent witnesses of evil deeds; we have been drenched by many storms; we have learnt the arts of equivocation and pretense; experience has made us suspicious of others and kept us from being truthful and open; intolerable conflicts have worn us down and even made us cynical. Are we still of any use?*[4]

In the words of Dietrich Bonhoeffer—the gentle young scholar who could have stayed at home with his books and his Bible, the pacifist who wept at war movies, the privileged young man who could have easily avoided danger—the answer can only be a resounding "yes."

ACKNOWLEDGMENTS

My first thank-you goes to Rev. Anna Levy-Lyons of the First Unitarian Church in Brooklyn, who introduced me to the words of Dietrich Bonhoeffer in a sermon before the United States' invasion of Iraq. At a time when I was questioning how I could protest the actions of my government, she told the story of a young minister who said that to do nothing in the face of evil was evil itself. I would also like to thank the authors Eric Metaxas and Charles Marsh, who wrote compelling narratives of Bonhoeffer. Their work was so important that I thought it had to be brought to the young readers and activists of today. Professor Marsh was exceptionally generous and encouraging about this book when I interviewed him about his work. I would also like to thank Dr. Ruth Tonkiss Cameron, the archivist at the Union Theological Seminary, for her warmth and kindness in talking to me about Bonhoeffer's time in the United States. Rev. Gottfried Brezger was welcoming and informative when I visited him at the Bonhoeffer home and gathering center in Berlin. And the docents at the Flossenbürg concentration camp pointed me to an obscure piece of scholarship suggesting that Dietrich Bonhoeffer was the first person to document the mass deportation of the Jews. I would especially like to thank Dr. David Gushee, Distinguished University Professor of Christian Ethics and director of the Center for Theology and Public Life at Mercer University, for his meticulous review of this manuscript before publication.

I am exceptionally lucky to have Alessandra Balzer as my editor and champion. Her impeccable editorial judgment and high standards inspire me to write books worthy of her list. Kelsey Murphy of HarperCollins was also enormous help: She worked tirelessly to find just the right images for the book and steered the manuscript through a painstaking process to ensure its accuracy. And I am just as lucky to have Heather Schroder as my agent. She is in my corner no matter what. I would also like to heartily thank Maya Packard and Bethany Reis for their rigorous and respectful copyediting. Rick Grand-Jean, my friend and a World War II aficionado, provided invaluable expertise.

As always, thanks to my husband, Paul, who played "groupie" when we traveled to Germany to research this book and who has always made my work possible, and my children, Brandon, Meaghan, and Matt, who make me want to do work that will make them proud.

TIMELINE

July 28, 1914—World War I begins.

June 28, 1919—The Treaty of Versailles is signed, ending World War I.

July 29, 1921—Adolf Hitler is elected leader of the new National Socialist Party, nicknamed the Nazi party.

April 1, 1924—Hitler is sentenced to prison for five years after the Nazis try to take over the German government. While in prison he writes his autobiography and his blueprint for the future of Germany, *Mein Kampf.*

1930–1931—Dietrich Bonhoeffer studies at Union Theological Seminary in New York.

January 30, 1933—Hitler wins election as chancellor of Germany after vowing to restore Germany to its former glory.

February 27, 1933—Hitler suspends the constitution, giving his storm troopers emergency powers to intercept private mail, listen in on phone conversations, and round up opponents, with no regard for legalities.

March 1933—The first concentration camp for "political prisoners" is established in Dachau.

April 1, 1933—Hitler announces a boycott of all Jewish-owned businesses.

April 22, 1933—Jews are banned from practicing medicine or law in state agencies.

April 25, 1933—Limits are put on the number of Jewish children who can attend school.

May 6, 1933—Jews are banned from teaching at universities.

May 10, 1933—Students burn thousands of "un-German" books.

September 28, 1933—Spouses of "non-Aryans" are banned from state employment.

September 29, 1933—Jews are barred from working in theater, film, and entertainment.

October, 1933—Jews are prohibited from being journalists, and all German newspapers are placed under Nazi control.

June 30–July 2, 1934—Night of the Long Knives. Hitler's men round up political opponents in midnight raids.

September 15, 1935—The Nuremberg Laws are passed, safe-guarding the purity of "German blood and German honor."

Marriage between "Aryans" and Jews are prohibited. Jews are stripped of their German citizenship.

December 1, 1936—All German children are required to join the Hitler Youth.

September 30, 1938—Germany takes over Czechoslovakian territory.

July 1939—Bonhoeffer flees to New York but immediately decides to return to Germany.

September 1, 1939—Germany invades Poland.

September 3, 1939—Great Britain and France declare war on Germany. World War II begins.

September 27, 1939—Poland surrenders. Hitler announces Germany will attack Belgium.

June 22, 1940—France surrenders to Germany.

April 1941—Germany conquers Yugoslavia, Greece, Albania, North Africa.

June 22, 1941—Germany invades Russia.

October 21, 1941—Bonhoeffer is one of the first to report the mass deportation of Jews to concentration camps.

September 1, 1941—Jews are required to wear the yellow Star of David.

January 20, 1942—The Final Solution for the extermination of the Jews is adopted.

June 1942—Bonhoeffer meets Maria von Wedemeyer.

August–September, 1942—Bonhoeffer assists in Operation 7, the escape of fourteen Jews to Switzerland.

November 2, 1942—British troops defeat German army in North Africa.

March 21, 1943—Rudolf-Christoph von Gersdorff attempts to assassinate Hitler with a pair of bombs hidden in his overcoat. Hitler leaves before the bombs can go off.

April 5, 1943—Bonhoeffer is arrested for financial irregularities associated with Operation 7.

July 1943—Allied troops land in Sicily.

September 1943—Allied troops land in Naples.

September 1943—Soviet troops defeat German troops in Kiev.

June 6, 1944—Allied troops land in Normandy, open a second front against Germany.

July 20, 1944—Claus von Stauffenberg places a bomb under the map table at Hitler's headquarters. The bomb goes off, killing four people; Hitler escapes relatively unhurt.

August 25, 1944—Paris is liberated. Allied troops arrive at German border.

December 1944—The Germans mount a final offensive, the Battle of the Bulge.

January 1945—The German retreat intensifies.

March 1945—Allied troops cross the Rhine and enter Germany.

April 1945—The Soviets encircle Berlin.

April 9, 1945—Bonhoeffer is executed at Flossenbürg
   concentration camp.

April 23, 1945—Flossenbürg is liberated.

April 30, 1945—Adolf Hitler commits suicide.

May 7–9, 1945—Germany surrenders.

ENDNOTES

Chapter Two: War Breaks Out

1. Sabine Leibholz-Bonhoeffer, *The Bonhoeffers: Portrait of a Family* (Chicago: Covenant Publications, 1994), 18.

Chapter Three: Bonhoeffer Seals His Destiny

1. Eberhard Bethge, *Dietrich Bonhoeffer: A Biography* (Minneapolis: Fortress, 2000), 37.
2. Charles Marsh, *Strange Glory: A Life of Dietrich Bonhoeffer* (New York: Alfred A. Knopf, 2014), 17.
3. Ibid.
4. Bethge, *Bonhoeffer*, 37.

Chapter Five: The Trip That Changed Everything

1. Marsh, *Strange Glory*, 30.
2. Ibid.

Chapter Eight: From Faith to Action

1. Bethge, *Bonhoeffer*, 109.

Chapter Nine: Grappling with the Existence of God

1. Marsh, *Strange Glory*, 94.
2. Bethge, *Bonhoeffer*, 143.

Chapter Ten: A Decisive Experience: Visiting the United States

1. *Dietrich Bonhoeffer Works*, ed. Clifford J. Greene, trans. Douglas W. Stott, vol. 10, *Barcelona, Berlin, New York, 1982–1931* (Minneapolis: Fortress, 2008), 294.
2. Bethge, *Bonhoeffer*, 116.
3. Ibid., 117.
4. Eric Metaxas, *Bonhoeffer: Pastor, Martyr, Prophet, Spy* (Nashville, Thomas Nelson, 2010), 109.
5. Ibid., 114.
6. Marsh, *Strange Glory*, 120.
7. "After Ten Years," essay by Dietrich Bonhoeffer, Christmas 1942.
8. Bethge, *Bonhoeffer*, 203.

Chapter Eleven: Heil, Hitler!

1. Marsh, *Strange Glory*, 151.
2. Metaxas, *Pastor, Martyr*, 125.
3. Ibid., 134.

Chapter Twelve: Speaking Out against the Führer

1. Marsh, *Strange Glory*, 160.
2. "Nazi Camp System," United States Holocaust Memorial Museum, http://www.ushmm.org/outreach/en/article .php?ModuleId=10007720.

Chapter Thirteen: The Aryan Paragraph

1. Marsh, *Strange Glory*, 165.
2. Metaxas, *Pastor, Martyr*, 154
3. Ibid, 143.
4. Marsh, *Strange Glory*, 176.
5. Bethge, *Bonhoeffer*, 257.

Chapter Fourteen: Committing Treason

1. "Timeline of Events: Anti-Jewish Boycott," United States Holocaust Memorial Museum, http://www.ushmm.org/ learn/timeline-of-events/1933-1938/anti-jewish-boycott.
2. Leibholz-Bonhoeffer, *The Bonhoeffers*, 75.

Chapter Fifteen: Bonfire of Hatred

1. Bethge, *Bonhoeffer*, 259.
2. Metaxas, *Pastor, Martyr*, 159.
3. "Facing History and Ourselves: Holocaust and Human Behavior, Introduction," quote from Adolf Hitler (1939), Facing History and Ourselves, https://www.facinghistory .org/for-educators/educator-resources/readings/school-barbarians.
4. Metaxas, *Pastor, Martyr*, 162.
5. Ibid.
6. Marsh, *Strange Glory*, 174.

Chapter Sixteen: A Nazi Church

1. Metaxas, *Pastor, Martyr*, 168.
2. Ibid., 165.
3. Ibid., 166.
4. Ibid., 193.
5. Ibid., 174.
6. Ibid., 171.
7. Ibid., 180.

Chapter Seventeen: A Different Kind of Resistance

1. Bethge, *Bonhoeffer*, 326.
2. Marsh, *Strange Glory*, 199.

Chapter Eighteen: Night of the Long Knives

1. Metaxas, *Pastor, Martyr,* 259.

2. Ibid., 248.

3. "Nuremberg Race Laws: Translation," United States Holocaust Memorial Museum, http://www.ushmm.org/ wlc/en/article.php?ModuleId=10007903.

Chapter Nineteen: A Breakaway Church

1. Bethge, *Bonhoeffer,* 411.

2. Metaxas, *Pastor, Martyr,* 259–60

3. Dietrich Bonhoeffer, *The Cost of Discipleship* (New York: Touchstone, 1995), 45.

4. Metaxas, *Pastor, Martyr,* 273.

Chapter Twenty: A Conspiracy Begins

1. "Nazi Persecution of the Disabled: Murder of the 'Unfit,'" United States Holocaust Memorial Museum, http://www .ushmm.org/information/exhibitions/online-features/ special-focus/nazi-persecution-of-the-disabled.

2. Eric Metaxas, *Bonhoeffer: The Life and Writings of Dietrich Bonhoeffer* (Nashville: Thomas Nelson, 2014), 59.

Chapter Twenty-One: The War Hits Home

1. Bethge, *Bonhoeffer*, 389.
2. Metaxas, *Pastor, Martyr*, 241; Marsh, *Strange Glory*, 213.
3. Metaxas, *Pastor, Martyr*, 242.

Chapter Twenty-Two: A Dark Night of the Soul

1. Ibid., 331.
2. Ruth Tonkiss Cameron (archivist, Union Theological Seminary), in discussion with the author, June 12, 2015.
3. Marsh, *Strange Glory*, 281.
4. Metaxas, *Pastor, Martyr*, 332.
5. Bethge, *Bonhoeffer*, 653.
6. Metaxas, *Pastor, Martyr*, 330.

Chapter Twenty-Three: From Clergyman to Courier

1. Ibid., 341.
2. Ibid., 343.
3. Ibid.
4. Dietrich Bonhoeffer, *Letters and Papers from Prison* (New York: Touchstone, 1997), 6.
5. "Stopping Genocide: The Responsibility to Protect," Thor Halvorssen, Human Rights Foundation, http://humanrightsfoundation.org/news/stopping-genocide-the-responsibility-to-protect-00263.

Chapter Twenty-Four: Undercover

1. Metaxas, *Pastor, Martyr*, 377.
2. Ibid., 404.
3. Ibid., 387.

Chapter Twenty-Five: Sounding the Alarm

1. Marsh, *Strange Glory*, 321.
2. Bethge, *Bonhoeffer*, 745.
3. Marsh, *Strange Glory*, 320–21.
4. "Reinhard Heydrich," Jewish Virtual Library, https://www. jewishvirtuallibrary.org/jsource/Holocaust/Heydrich.html.
5. Ibid.
6. Roseman, Mark, *The Wansee Conference and the Final Solution: A Reconsideration* (New York: Picador, 2003), 148.

Chapter Twenty-Six: Love in Wartime

1. Metaxas, *Pastor, Martyr*, 393.

Chapter Twenty-Seven: The Noose Grows Tighter

1. Marsh, *Strange Glory*, 338–39.
2. Bethge, *Bonhoeffer*, 771.
3. Marsh, *Strange Glory*, 332.

Chapter Twenty-Nine: Caught

1. Metaxas, *Pastor, Martyr*, 436.
2. Bethge, *Bonhoeffer*, 831.
3. Metaxas, *Pastor, Martyr*, 439.
4. Bethge, *Bonhoeffer*, 811.
5. Ibid., 24.
6. Metaxas, *Pastor, Martyr*, 456.

Chapter Thirty: Another Attempt on Hitler's Life

1. Ibid., 481.

Chapter Thirty-One: Evidence of Treason

1. Bethge, *Bonhoeffer*, 939.
2. Metaxas, *Pastor, Martyr*, 486.
3. Ibid., 492.
4. Bethge, *Bonhoeffer*, 832.

Chapter Thirty-Three: Eternity at Last

1. *Flossenbürg Concentration Camp 1938–1945: Catalogue of the Permanent Exhibition*, 41.
2. Author notes, visit to Flossenbürg concentration camp, March 2015.
3. Bethge, *Bonhoeffer*, 928.

Epilogue

1. Metaxas, *Pastor, Martyr*, 537.

Author's Note

1. Elizabeth Sifton and Fritz Stern, *No Ordinary Men: Dietrich Bonhoeffer and Hans von Dohnanyi, Resisters Against Hitler in Church and State* (New York: New York Review Books, 2013), 102.

2. The King Center, http://www.thekingcenter.org/archive.

3. Metaxas, *Pastor, Martyr*, 154.

4. *Dietrich Bonhoeffer Works*, ed. John W. de Gruchy, trans. Isabel Best, Lisa E. Dahill, Reinhard Krauss, Nancy Lukens, vol. 8, *Letters and Papers from Prison* (Minneapolis: Fortress, 2009), 52.

SELECTED BIBLIOGRAPHY

Bethge, Eberhard. *Dietrich Bonhoeffer, A Biography.*
Minneapolis: Fortress, 2000.

Bonhoeffer, Dietrich. *Letters and Papers from Prison.* New
York: Touchstone, 1997.

Facing History and Ourselves: www.facinghistory.org.

*Flossenbürg Concentration Camp 1938–1945, Catalogue
of the Permanent Exhibition.* Flossenbürg, Germany:
Flossenbürg Memorial Foundation, 2009.

Leibholz-Bonhoeffer, Sabine. *The Bonhoeffers: Portrait of a
Family.* Chicago: Covenant Publications, 1994.

Marsh, Charles. *Strange Glory: A Life of Dietrich Bonhoeffer.*
New York: Alfred A. Knopf, 2014.

Metaxas, Eric. *Bonhoeffer: Pastor, Martyr, Prophet, Spy.* Nashville: Thomas Nelson, 2010.

Sifton, Elizabeth and Fritz Stern. *No Ordinary Men: Dietrich Bonhoeffer and Hans von Dohnanyi, Resisters Against Hitler in Church and State.* New York: New York Review Books, 2013.

United States Holocaust Memorial Museum: www.ushmm.org.

INTERVIEWS

Cameron, Ruth Tonkiss, archivist, Union Theological Seminary, New York, NY. In discussion with the author. July 2015.

Marsh, Charles, author, *Strange Glory: A Life of Dietrich Bonhoeffer* and professor of religious studies, University of Virginia. In discussion with the author. June 17, 2015.

Scheffler, Rev. Burckhard, director, Bonhoeffer Haus, Berlin. In discussion with the author. March 17, 2015.

OTHER SOURCES

United States Holocaust Memorial Museum archives

Berlin State Library

Flossenbürg concentration camp archives

INDEX